Grade 6

Scott Foresman

Grammar and Writing Practice Book

Editorial Offices: Glenview, Illinois • Parsippany, New Jersey • New York, New York
Sales Offices: Boston, Massachusetts • Duluth, Georgia • Glenview, Illinois
Coppell, Texas • Sacramento, California • Mesa, Arizona

ISBN: 0-328-14627-7

Copyright © Pearson Education, Inc.

All Rights Reserved. Printed in the United States of America. This publication, or parts thereof, may be used with appropriate equipment to reproduce copies for classroom use only.

23 24 25 26 27 28 V0N4 19 18 17 16 15 14

Unit 1 Loyalty and Respect

WEEK 1 Old Yeller
Four Kinds of Sentences 1

WEEK 2 Mother Fletcher's Gift
Subjects and Predicates 5

WEEK 3 Viva New Jersey
Independent and Dependent Clauses 9

WEEK 4 Saving the Rainforests
Compound and Complex Sentences 13

WEEK 5 When Crowbar Came
Common and Proper Nouns 17

Unit 2 Space and Time

WEEK 1 The Universe
Regular and Irregular Plural Nouns 21

WEEK 2 Dinosaur Ghosts: The Mystery of *Coelophysis*
Possessive Nouns 25

WEEK 3 A Week in the 1800s
Action and Linking Verbs 29

WEEK 4 Good-bye to the Moon
Subject-Verb Agreement 33

WEEK 5 Egypt
Past, Present, and Future Tenses 37

Unit 3 Challenges and Obstacles

WEEK 1 Hatchet
Principal Parts of Regular Verbs 41

WEEK 2 When Marian Sang
Principal Parts of Irregular Verbs 45

WEEK 3 Learning to Swim
Verbs, Objects, and Subject Complements 49

WEEK 4 Juan Verdades: The Man Who Couldn't Tell a Lie
Troublesome Verbs 53

WEEK 5 Elizabeth Blackwell: Medical Pioneer
Prepositions 57

Grammar and Writing Practice Book

Unit 4 Explorers, Pioneers, and Discoverers

WEEK 1 Into the Ice
Subject and Object Pronouns 61

WEEK 2 The Chimpanzees I Love
Pronouns and Antecedents 65

WEEK 3 Black Frontiers
Possessive Pronouns 69

WEEK 4 Space Cadets
Indefinite and Reflexive Pronouns 73

WEEK 5 Inventing the Future: A Photobiography of Thomas Alva Edison
Using *Who* and *Whom* 77

Unit 5 Resources

WEEK 1 The View from Saturday
Contractions and Negatives 81

WEEK 2 Harvesting Hope: The Story of Cesar Chavez
Adjectives and Articles 85

WEEK 3 The River That Went to the Sky: A Story from Malawi
Demonstrative Adjectives 89

WEEK 4 Gold
Comparative and Superlative Adjectives 93

WEEK 5 The House of Wisdom
Adverbs 97

Unit 6 Exploring Cultures

WEEK 1 Don Quixote and the Windmills
Modifiers 101

WEEK 2 Ancient Greece
Conjunctions 105

WEEK 3 The All-American Slurp
Commas 109

WEEK 4 The Aztec News
Quotations and Quotation Marks 113

WEEK 5 Where Opportunity Awaits
Punctuation 117

Grammar Extra Practice

Four Kinds of Sentences	**122**
Subjects and Predicates	**123**
Independent and Dependent Clauses	**124**
Compound and Complex Sentences	**125**
Common and Proper Nouns	**126**
Regular and Irregular Plural Nouns	**127**
Possessive Nouns	**128**
Action and Linking Verbs	**129**
Subject-Verb Agreement	**130**
Past, Present, and Future Tenses	**131**
Principal Parts of Regular Verbs	**132**
Principal Parts of Irregular Verbs	**133**
Verbs, Objects, and Subject Complements	**134**
Troublesome Verbs	**135**
Prepositions	**136**
Subject and Object Pronouns	**137**
Pronouns and Antecedents	**138**
Possessive Pronouns	**139**
Indefinite and Reflexive Pronouns	**140**
Using *Who* and *Whom*	**141**
Contractions and Negatives	**142**
Adjectives and Articles	**143**
Demonstrative Adjectives	**144**
Comparative and Superlative Adjectives	**145**
Adverbs	**146**
Modifiers	**147**
Conjunctions	**148**
Commas	**149**
Quotations and Quotation Marks	**150**
Punctuation	**151**

Standardized Test Preparation

UNITS 1–2	Language Test	**153**
	Writing Test	**154**
UNITS 3–4	Language Test	**155**
	Writing Test	**156**
UNITS 5–6	Language Test	**157**
	Writing Test	**158**

Unit Writing Lessons

UNIT 1 — **PERSONAL NARRATIVE**
- Notes for a Personal Narrative **160**
- Write a Strong Story Opener **161**
- Elaboration: Combine Sentences **162**
- Self-Evaluation Guide **163**

UNIT 2 — **HOW-TO REPORT**
- How-to Chart **164**
- Time-Order Words **165**
- Elaboration: Use Strong Verbs **166**
- Self-Evaluation Guide **167**

UNIT 3 — **COMPARE AND CONTRAST ESSAY**
- Venn Diagram **168**
- Words That Compare and Contrast **169**
- Elaboration: Prepositional Phrases **170**
- Self-Evaluation Guide **171**

UNIT 4	**STORY**	
	Story Chart	**172**
	Good Beginnings	**173**
	Elaboration: Using *Who* and *Whom*	**174**
	Self-Evaluation Guide	**175**

UNIT 5	**PERSUASIVE ARGUMENT**	
	Persuasion Chart	**176**
	Persuasive Words	**177**
	Elaboration: Adjectives	**178**
	Self-Evaluation Guide	**179**

UNIT 6	**RESEARCH REPORT**	
	K-W-L Chart	**180**
	Topic and Detail Sentences	**181**
	Elaboration: Modifiers	**182**
	Self-Evaluation Guide	**183**

Grammar Lessons

Name _____

Old Yeller

DEVELOP THE CONCEPT

Four Kinds of Sentences

> A **declarative sentence**, or statement, tells something. It ends with a period.
>   Joey is reading the autobiography of his favorite baseball player.
> An **interrogative sentence** asks a question. It ends with a question mark.
>   Have you ever written a story about your life?
> An **imperative sentence** gives a command or makes a request. It ends with a period. *You* is the understood subject.
>   Keep a journal of your daily adventures.
> An **exclamatory sentence** shows strong feeling. It ends with an exclamation mark.
>   How funny my autobiography would be!
> An **interjection** is a word or a group of words that expresses strong feeling. It is not a complete sentence.
>   Wow! Hooray! Ouch!

Directions Write *D* if the sentence is declarative. Write *IN* if the sentence is interrogative. Write *IM* if the sentence is imperative. Write *E* if the sentence is exclamatory.

1. Many famous people have pets. _____
2. What is a pet license? _____
3. Find the groomer's number in the phone book. _____
4. You can adopt a pet from an animal shelter. _____
5. Wow! I never knew Spot could run so fast! _____

Directions Put a period, a question mark, or an exclamation mark at the end of each sentence to show what kind of sentence it is.

6. Have you taken the dog for a walk _____
7. My mom plans to surprise my dad with a new puppy _____
8. Oh, no! The lizard escaped from his tank _____
9. Megan's baby sister is allergic to dogs and cats _____
10. How did your kitten climb onto our roof _____

Home Activity Your child learned about the four different kinds of sentences. Have your child name the four kinds of sentences and write an example of each one.

Grammar and Writing Practice Book Unit 1 Week 1 **Day 2** **1**

Name _____

Old Yeller

APPLY TO WRITING

Four Kinds of Sentences

Directions Change each declarative sentence into an interrogative sentence. Don't forget the proper capitalization and end mark.

1. Pablo's mother is a dog trainer.

   _____

2. Our family would enjoy visiting the zoo.

   _____

3. The main character of the story is a dog.

   _____

4. Soomin's pet rabbit has had babies.

   _____

5. Jacob has taught his dog to roll over.

   _____

6. Sarah will take the dog for a run.

   _____

Directions Choose a topic, such as a pet, a bike, new clothes, or a type of food. Write a declarative, an interrogative, an imperative, and an exclamatory sentence about this topic.

7. _____

   _____

8. _____

   _____

9. _____

   _____

10. _____

Home Activity Your child learned how to write the four different kinds of sentences. Ask your child to find an example of each kind of sentence in a favorite book.

2 Unit 1 Week 1 **Day 3**   **Grammar and Writing Practice Book**

Name _____

Independent and Dependent Clauses

> An **independent clause** has a subject and verb and can stand alone as a complete sentence. A **dependent clause** has a subject and a verb but cannot stand alone as a complete sentence. In the following sentences, the independent clause is underlined once; the dependent clause is underlined twice. The dependent clause is followed by a comma when it comes before the independent clause.
>
> Lucinda took the dog home because she was lonely.
> Because she was lonely, Lucinda took the dog home.

Directions Write *IC* after each independent clause and *DC* after each dependent clause.

1. Because she was friendly. _____
2. Lucinda ran to the basement and found it empty. _____
3. Jan bathed Shadow in the backyard. _____
4. When the power went out. _____
5. After they crossed the Mississippi River. _____
6. If Carmen had not seen it. _____
7. Tenants mingled outside their apartments. _____
8. The boys won the baseball game. _____
9. As she called from the window. _____
10. They were eating dinner. _____

Directions Underline the independent clause and circle the dependent clause in each sentence.

11. Because the dog was abandoned, Lucinda had to take care of him.
12. The dog caused problems when it ran away.
13. Although she was shy, Lucinda talked to Ashley.
14. While Lucinda was gone, her parents almost called the police.
15. Ashley read many books because she wanted to be a writer.

Home Activity Your child learned about independent and dependent clauses. Have your child tell you what independent and dependent clauses are and give you an example of each.

Grammar and Writing Practice Book

Independent and Dependent Clauses

Directions Add an independent clause to each dependent clause to make a complete sentence.

1. When I went to the store, _____

2. Although Henry didn't feel well, _____

3. When Maria thought about Cuba, _____

4. While we were on vacation, _____

5. After the test was over, _____

6. Before I could raise my hand, _____

7. Because Michael broke his leg, _____

8. Until I finish my homework, _____

9. Although it was sunny, _____

10. Unless we ride our bikes, _____

Directions Add a dependent clause to each independent clause to make it more interesting.

11. _____
_____ , Thomas raced down the stairs.

12. Ashley decided to walk to school _____
_____

13. She was sad _____

14. _____ Mom walks a mile.

Home Activity Your child learned how to use independent and dependent clauses in writing. Have your child write a sentence about his or her favorite animal using an independent clause and a dependent clause.

Name _____

Saving the Rain Forests

DEVELOP THE CONCEPT

Compound and Complex Sentences

> A **simple sentence** has a complete subject and a complete predicate.
> The clouds gathered quickly.
> A **compound sentence** has two or more simple sentences joined by a comma and a conjunction such as *and, but,* or *or.*
> The clouds gathered quickly, and the leaves rustled in the wind.
> A **complex sentence** has one independent clause and one or more dependent clauses.
> Although it was sunny just a moment ago, the clouds gathered quickly.
> A **compound-complex sentence** has more than one independent clause and at least one dependent clause.
> Although it was sunny just a moment ago, the clouds gathered quickly, and the leaves rustled in the wind.

Directions Identify each sentence as *simple, compound, complex,* or *compound-complex.*

1. The forest ranger is speaking at my school, and I can't wait to hear him. _____

2. When it rains, it pours. _____

3. When they got back from the boat tour, Donna took a nap, and Terry read the paper. _____

4. Paul looked up at the tree, and he saw a huge fern. _____

5. Many species of plants and animals live in the rain forest. _____

6. Although I have a map, I can't find the camp. _____

Directions Complete each compound sentence with the conjunction *and, but,* or *or.*

7. She loved to hike, _____ she loved to camp.

8. Some animals live among the leaves, _____ some live on the tree trunks.

9. We must protect the rain forests, _____ they will disappear.

10. Larry loved the rain, _____ Darla did not.

11. Forest fires are common, _____ they endanger the rain forest.

12. You need to hurry, _____ I'll leave you behind.

Home Activity Your child learned about compound and complex sentences. Have your child tell you what compound and complex sentences are. Then ask your child to find one example of each kind of sentence in a magazine article.

Grammar and Writing Practice Book   Unit 1 Week 4 **Day 2** **13**

Name _____

Compound and Complex Sentences

Saving the Rain Forests

APPLY TO WRITING

Directions Join each pair of simple sentences to make a compound sentence. Use a comma and a conjunction such as *and, but,* or *or.*

1. Water from the trees creates clouds.
   The water in the clouds falls back as rain.

   _____

   _____

2. Shut the window.
   The basement might flood.

   _____

   _____

3. Mining is an important industry in the area.
   It has damaged the rain forest.

   _____

   _____

4. The insect might be harmless.
   We decided not to touch it.

   _____

   _____

Directions Add an independent clause to each dependent clause to make a complex sentence.

5. Although we could not see them, _____

   _____

6. When the medicine arrived, _____

   _____

7. While Jack slept, _____

   _____

8. After we ate dinner at the campsite, _____

   _____

Home Activity Your child learned how to use compound and complex sentences in writing. Have your child choose a simple sentence from a book and rewrite it first to make a compound sentence and then to make a complex sentence.

14 Unit 1 Week 4 Day 3   **Grammar and Writing Practice Book**

Name _____

When Crowbar Came

DEVELOP THE CONCEPT

Common and Proper Nouns

> A **common noun** names any person, place, or thing.
>
> The shiny <u>coins</u> jingled in his <u>pocket</u>.
>
> A **proper noun** names a particular person, place, or thing. When a proper noun is more than one word, capitalize only the important word or words.
>
> Her cousin lives in <u>South America</u>. <u>Aunt Jean</u> visited the <u>Statue of Liberty</u>.
>
> Some proper nouns, including titles for people, have short forms called abbreviations that begin with capital letters and end with periods.
>
> <u>Gen.</u> Jones visited the middle school. I met Edward Wu, <u>Jr.</u>

Directions Underline the proper nouns and circle the common nouns.

1. Dr. Tee Van chuckled at the bird.

2. My uncle put his money in the National State Bank.

3. Aunt Louise worked in her garden.

4. Mrs. George just became an aunt.

5. Our neighbors moved from Maine to Oregon.

   Dad and Rev. Johnson had lunch on Saturday.

   She bought presents for Aunt Sue.

8. May I have more broccoli, Mom?

Directions Rewrite the proper nouns using correct capitalization, punctuation, and abbreviations when possible.

9. doctor martin luther king, junior _____

10. general forrester _____

11. doctor bart from boston _____

12. reverend smith _____

Home Activity Your child learned about common nouns and proper nouns. Have your child tell you the difference between common nouns and proper nouns and find examples of each in a magazine.

Grammar and Writing Practice Book   Unit 1 Week 5 **Day 2**   **17**

Name _____

When Crowbar Came

APPLY TO WRITING

Common and Proper Nouns

Directions Write a sentence using a common noun and a proper noun, as indicated, for the words in ( ).

Example: (name, P/animal, C) *Kirby is my dog.*

1. (relative, P/food, C) _____
2. (country, P/season, C) _____
3. (friend, P /vehicle, C) _____
4. (title, P /hobby, C) _____
5. (holiday, P /clothing, C) _____

Directions Rewrite the sentences using correct capitalization for proper nouns.

6. bobby attends turner middle school in wellston, iowa.

   _____

7. crowbar stayed with the georges for two-and-a-half years.

   _____

8. twig's test is scheduled for next tuesday.

   _____

9. the harvest bakery sells pumpkin pies only in november.

   _____

10. last year luke and his friends visited the statue of liberty.

    _____

11. i drove my cousin to union station.

    _____

12. ms. roberts lives on beale street.

    _____

Home Activity Your child learned how to use common and proper nouns in writing. Ask your child to write sentences describing your community. Then have your child underline the common nouns and circle the proper nouns he or she used.

18 Unit 1 Week 5 **Day 3** **Grammar and Writing Practice Book**

Name _____

When Crowbar Came

TEST PREPARATION

Common and Proper Nouns

Directions Mark the letter that lists the proper nouns in each sentence.

1. One Saturday in September, a crow arrived at our door.
   - **A** morning, September
   - **B** Saturday, crow
   - **C** Saturday, September
   - **D** crow, door

2. The Midwest is part of the United States.
   - **A** Midwest, part
   - **B** United States
   - **C** Midwest, States
   - **D** Midwest, United States

3. Captain John sailed down the Hudson River.
   - **A** Captain John, Hudson River
   - **B** Captain John, sailed
   - **C** John, Hudson
   - **D** Captain, River

4. My sister Pam works at a bank in town.
   - **A** Pam, bank, town
   - **B** My, Pam
   - **C** Pam
   - **D** sister, Pam, bank, town

Directions Mark the letter that lists the common nouns in each sentence.

5. The Georges owned a red fox named Fulva.
   - **A** The Georges, Fulva
   - **B** Georges, fox
   - **C** Georges, Fulva
   - **D** fox

6. A group of mothers worked at Mercy Hospital.
   - **A** group, mothers, Mercy Hospital
   - **B** group, mothers
   - **C** group, Mercy Hospital
   - **D** mothers, Mercy Hospital

7. During our conversation, Mr. Ori drank tea.
   - **A** conversation, tea
   - **B** Mr. Ori, tea
   - **C** conversation, Ori, tea
   - **D** conversation, Mr., tea

8. Before winter, birds begin their migration.
   - **A** winter, birds
   - **B** winter
   - **C** winter, birds, migration
   - **D** winter, birds, their

Home Activity Your child prepared for taking tests on common and proper nouns. With your child, find four examples each of common and proper nouns in a newspaper article.

Grammar and Writing Practice Book   Unit 1 Week 5 Day 4   **19**

Name _____

When Crowbar Came
CUMULATIVE REVIEW

Common and Proper Nouns

Directions Write *P* if the underlined noun is a proper noun. Write *C* if it is a common noun.

1. My <u>dad</u> knocked over the bird's nest. _____
2. The <u>park</u> in the Bronx has a steep slide. _____
3. <u>Luke</u> found the bird in a spruce. _____
4. <u>Hamburger</u> was his favorite food. _____
5. Do you live in <u>Lake Placid</u>? _____
6. <u>Crowbar</u> marched around like a military general. _____

Directions Underline the proper nouns and circle the common nouns.

7. The boy found the bird on Halloween.
8. Uncle Ron brought some birdseed.
9. Grandpa Ruiz drove to New York from Tennessee.
10. In summer, warm breezes rustle the leaves in the oaks.
11. Craig opened an account at First National Bank.
12. Mrs. George writes stories on her typewriter.
13. In September, the trees turn many colors.
14. Dr. Kalmbach wrote a report about farmers and crows.
15. The director of the Bronx Zoo visited the Georges.

Directions Replace the common nouns in ( ) with proper nouns. Be sure to use appropriate capitalization.

16. My (relative) _____ has never been to (continent) _____.
17. (title) _____ Arthur Chin was born in (country) _____.
18. Luke's friend (name) _____ works for (company) _____.
19. (school) _____ is closed on (date) _____.
20. (city) _____ is in (state) _____.

Home Activity Your child reviewed common nouns and proper nouns. With your child, find three common nouns and three proper nouns in a printed advertisement.

20 Unit 1 Week 5 **Day 5** Grammar and Writing Practice Book

Name _____

The Universe
DEVELOP THE CONCEPT

Regular and Irregular Plural Nouns

> **Plural nouns** name more than one person, place, or thing.
> - Most plural nouns are formed by adding *-s*.
>   swing/swings   animal/animals   boy/boys
> - Add *-es* to nouns ending in *ch, sh, x, z, s,* and *ss*.
>   fox/foxes   bush/bushes   church/churches
> - If a noun ends in a consonant and *y*, change *y* to *i* and add *-es*.
>   blueberry/blueberries   pony/ponies   penny/pennies
> - Some nouns have **irregular plural** forms. They change spelling.
>   man/men   tooth/teeth   child/children   foot/feet
> - For most nouns that end in *f* or *fe*, change *f* to *v* and add *-es*.
>   half/halves   wolf/wolves   thief/thieves   shelf/shelves
> - Some nouns have the same singular and plural forms.
>   salmon   trout   sheep   moose   deer
> - For compound nouns, make only the important word plural.
>   mothers-in-law   commanders-in-chief
> - When a noun ends in a vowel and *o*, add *-s*: *video/videos, radio/radios*.
> - Check a dictionary for plurals of nouns ending in a consonant and *o*: *photo/photos, potato/potatoes, tomato/tomatoes, hero/heroes*.

Directions Write the plural form of the noun in parentheses.

1. They tuned their _____ (radio) to the Space Ranger Show.
2. How many _____ (mystery) does our universe hold?
3. My brother likes to read about space _____ (hero).
4. Casey had model rockets on all of his _____ (shelf).
5. Space telescopes are able to transmit amazing _____ (image).
6. Ian packed his astronomy books in _____ (box).
7. Mrs. Peck divided the class into _____ (half).
8. All of the _____ (chairman) met at the space summit.
9. Alan has seen three space shuttle _____ (launch).
10. Ellen searched three _____ (library) for books on quasars.

Home Activity Your child learned about regular and irregular plural nouns. With your child, look at labels on food products. Ask him or her to identify regular and irregular plural nouns.

Grammar and Writing Practice Book   Unit 2 Week 1 Day 2   **21**

Name _____

APPLY TO WRITING — The Universe

Regular and Irregular Plural Nouns

Directions Write a sentence using the plural form of each given noun.

1. country
   _____

2. beach
   _____

3. tooth
   _____

4. video
   _____

5. porch
   _____

6. story
   _____

7. leaf
   _____

8. secretary of state
   _____

9. child
   _____

10. life
    _____

Home Activity Your child learned how to write regular and irregular plural nouns. Have your child point out plural nouns on packages and labels and explain the rule for forming each plural.

22 Unit 2 Week 1 **Day 3** **Grammar and Writing Practice Book**

Name _____

The Universe

TEST PREPARATION

Regular and Irregular Plural Nouns

Directions Circle the letter of the plural form of each underlined noun.

1. The telescope was a great <u>discovery</u>.
   - A discoverys
   - B discovery
   - C discovery's
   - D discoveries

2. Michael framed a <u>photo</u> of the space shuttle Columbia.
   - A photos
   - B photo
   - C photoes
   - D photos'

3. The title of the novel is <u>Sheep</u> in Space.
   - A *Sheeps*
   - B *Sheepes*
   - C *Sheep*
   - D *sheep*

4. While stargazing, Jan and Kurt saw a <u>moose</u>.
   - A moose
   - B moose'
   - C mooses
   - D moose's

5. On Tucker's <u>ranch</u>, we could see millions of stars.
   - A ranchs
   - B ranches
   - C ranch
   - D ranch's

6. Betsy named the <u>calf</u> Milky Way.
   - A calfs
   - B calves
   - C calfes
   - D calve's

7. How much would the <u>child</u> weigh on Mars?
   - A child
   - B childs
   - C childrens
   - D children

8. Scientists do not measure space by the <u>foot</u>.
   - A foots
   - B feets
   - C feet
   - D foots'

9. In what <u>century</u> did Galileo live?
   - A centuries
   - B centurys
   - C centuries'
   - D century's

10. Matt earned his space ranger <u>patch</u>.
    - A patchs
    - B patches
    - C patch
    - D patchs'

Home Activity Your child prepared for taking tests on regular and irregular plural nouns. Have your child make flash cards with singular and plural forms of nouns on opposite sides. Use the cards to help him or her learn plural forms.

Grammar and Writing Practice Book   Unit 2 Week 1 **Day 4** **23**

Name _____

The Universe
CUMULATIVE REVIEW

Regular and Irregular Plural Nouns

Directions Write the plural form of the noun.

1. shoe _____
2. wrist _____
3. knife _____
4. strawberry _____
5. fox _____
6. wife _____
7. wish _____
8. father-in-law _____
9. zoo _____
10. potato _____

Directions Circle the correct plural form of the nouns in parentheses.

11. One of my (wishes/wish's) is to be an astronaut.

12. A group of (ladys/ladies) from Iowa toured the space center.

13. Fifteen (childs/children) rode a bus to space camp.

14. Alex builds model space (shuttles/shuttle's).

15. Three (deer/deers) ate by moonlight.

16. The day of the moon landing was the best day of their (lifes/lives).

17. The telescope stood two (foots/feet) from the ground.

18. Audrey has a collection of Jupiter (photos/photoes).

19. My brother doesn't appreciate the (mysterys/mysteries) of the universe.

20. Neither of my (sister-in-laws/sisters-in-law) could locate the North Star.

Home Activity Your child reviewed regular and irregular plural nouns. Ask your child to list things you have in your kitchen and write the plural form for each noun.

24 Unit 2 Week 1 **Day 5** **Grammar and Writing Practice Book**

Name _____

Dinosaur Ghosts
DEVELOP THE CONCEPT

Possessive Nouns

> A **possessive noun** shows ownership. A **singular possessive noun** shows that one person, place, or thing has or owns something. A **plural possessive noun** shows that more than one person, place, or thing has or owns something.
>
> - To make a singular noun show possession, add an apostrophe (') and -s.
>   a dinosaur's bones   Sis's hat
> - To make a plural noun that ends in -s show possession, add an apostrophe (').
>   many dinosaurs' bones   the Jonses' house
> - To make a plural noun that does not end in -s show possession, add an apostrophe (') and -s.
>   the men's tools   many sheep's wool

Directions Write each noun as a possessive noun. Write *S* if the possessive noun is singular. Write *P* if the possessive noun is plural.

1. parents _____ _____
2. photo _____ _____
3. child _____ _____
4. Miss Meyer _____ _____
5. stores _____ _____
6. country _____ _____
7. James _____ _____
8. teeth _____ _____

Directions Add an apostrophe (') or an apostrophe (') and -s to make the underlined nouns possessive. Write the possessive noun on the line.

9. <u>Ghost Ranch</u> hills looked red and green. _____

10. The <u>reptiles</u> deaths mystified the scientists. _____

11. <u>Animals</u> red blood cells carry oxygen. _____

12. The <u>herd</u> young were left behind. _____

13. The <u>predator</u> teeth were long and sharp. _____

14. The <u>dinosaurs</u> necks were curved and twisted. _____

Home Activity Your child learned about possessive nouns. Together read a newspaper or magazine article. Have your child find and circle three singular and three plural possessive nouns in the article.

Grammar and Writing Practice Book   Unit 2 Week 2 **Day 2**   **25**

Name _____

Dinosaur Ghosts

APPLY TO WRITING

Possessive Nouns

Directions Change the underlined words to a possessive noun. Write the new sentence.

1. The <u>edges of the knives</u> were dull from cutting rope.
   _____
   _____

2. The <u>attention of the students</u> was drawn away from the exhibit.
   _____
   _____

3. The <u>large eyes of the creature</u> were helpful for finding prey.
   _____
   _____

4. The <u>rays of the sun</u> scorched the Earth.
   _____
   _____

5. Have you ever seen <u>the beautiful canyons of New Mexico</u>?
   _____
   _____

6. The <u>discoveries of the scientists</u> were on display.
   _____
   _____

7. There were pools of water along the <u>edge of the river</u>.
   _____
   _____

8. The <u>eruption of the volcano</u> shook the Earth.
   _____
   _____

Home Activity Your child learned how to use possessive nouns in writing. Write the words *child, children, girl, girls, baby,* and *babies* on paper. Have your child write sentences using the possessive forms of the words.

Name _____

Dinosaur Ghosts
TEST PREPARATION

Possessive Nouns

Directions Mark the word that completes the sentence.

1. My _____ passion is prehistoric life.
   A teachers
   B teacher
   C teachers's
   D teacher's

2. _____ collection of bones was discovered in New Mexico.
   A Charles Camp's
   B Charles's Camp
   C Charles Camps'
   D Charles Camps

3. The _____ art projects were all about dinosaurs.
   A childrens
   B children's
   C childrens'
   D childs'

4. Get _____ tools out of the rain!
   A Nicks'
   B Nicks
   C Nick's
   D Nick

5. The Triassic period is part of the _____ history.
   A Earths'
   B Earth
   C Earth's
   D Earths's

6. _____ teeth are suited for eating meat.
   A Carnivores
   B Carnivore
   C Carnivores'
   D Carnivore's

7. The _____ sneeze disrupted the fossils.
   A technician's
   B technicians'
   C technicians's
   D technician

8. _____ class was studying phytosaurs.
   A Mrs. Graves'
   B Mrs. Graves
   C Mrs. Graves's
   D Mrs. Graveses

Home Activity Your child prepared for taking tests on possessive nouns. Write the word *dinosaur*, *reptiles*, and *men* on paper. Ask your child to write the possessive forms of the words and to explain how he or she did so.

Grammar and Writing Practice Book   Unit 2 Week 2 **Day 4** **27**

Name _____

Dinosaur Ghosts

CUMULATIVE REVIEW

Possessive Nouns

Directions Write each noun as a possessive noun. Write *S* if the possessive noun is singular. Write *P* if the possessive noun is plural.

1. dinosaurs   _____   _____
2. night   _____   _____
3. bone   _____   _____
4. mothers   _____   _____
5. feet   _____   _____

Directions Circle the correct possessive noun in ( ) to complete each sentence.

6. The dinosaur discoveries are the (ranchs', ranch's) claim to fame.

7. The (men's, mens') examination of fossils took two days.

8. Curt read about the (phytosaur', phytosaur's) tail.

9. The class watched a video about three (paleontologists', paleontologist's) findings.

10. Do you want to be (Dr. Colberts', Dr. Colbert's) assistant?

Directions Write each sentence. Change the underlined phrase to show possession.

11. The diary of Charles Camp held a record of his findings.
_____

12. The red hue of the rocks looked eerie at night.
_____

13. A group of young scientists filled the buses of the school.
_____

14. The cracks of the skeletons were clearly visible.
_____

15. The events of the day excited the crew.
_____

Home Activity Your child reviewed possessive nouns. Point to single and multiple objects in your home and have your child say and spell the possessive forms of the names.

28 Unit 2 Week 2 **Day 5**   **Grammar and Writing Practice Book**

Name _____

A Week in the 1800s

DEVELOP THE CONCEPT

Action and Linking Verbs

> A **verb** is the main word in the predicate of a sentence. The verb tells what the subject of the sentence is or does. An **action verb** tells what the subject does. A **linking verb** links, or joins, the subject with a word or words in the predicate that tell what the subject is or is like. Linking verbs are forms of *be*, such as *am, is, are, was,* and *were. Become, seem, appear, feel, taste, smell,* and *look* can be linking verbs.
>
> **Action Verbs**   Grandma <u>scrubs</u> the wooden floor. We <u>pump</u> water.
>
> **Linking Verbs**   The bread <u>smells</u> wonderful. He <u>is</u> hungry.
>
> - A **predicate nominative** is a noun or pronoun that follows a linking verb and identifies or explains the subject: *Sarah's brother was the <u>leader</u> on his team.*

Directions Write *A* if the underlined word is an action verb. Write *L* if the underlined word is a linking verb. Write *PN* if the underlined word is a predicate nominative.

1. The apples <u>were</u> crunchy.   _____

2. We <u>serve</u> the bread with fresh butter.   _____

3. Erika is their <u>neighbor</u>.   _____

4. Hot coals <u>heat</u> the iron.   _____

5. Erika <u>became</u> impatient with the boys.   _____

Directions Underline each action verb. Circle each linking verb.

6. We passed the hot bread around the table.

7. Matthew is hungry, and supper smells delicious.

8. Farmers used every part of the corn plant.

9. Amy feels sad about the death of the chicken.

10. Jay feels the hot sun on his face.

11. Erika was ready for her chores.

12. The boys worked steadily until sunset.

13. The stranger at the farm looked suspicious.

14. The oven seemed hot enough, so Sarah shoved the bread in.

Home Activity Your child learned about action and linking verbs. Describe what a family member looks like and does. Say the sentences slowly and have your child identify the action and linking verbs you use.

Grammar and Writing Practice Book   Unit 2 Week 3 **Day 2** **29**

Name _____

A Week in the 1800s

APPLY TO WRITING

Action and Linking Verbs

Directions Add your own action verb to complete each sentence. Write the sentence on the lines.

1. Women _____ the clothes with homemade soap.
   _____
   _____

2. Amanda _____ to school because there were no buses.
   _____
   _____

3. The girls _____ long hours in the hot kitchen.
   _____
   _____

4. Alex _____ his finger when he touched the hot metal.
   _____
   _____

5. The blacksmith's apprentice _____ the trade by watching and practicing.
   _____
   _____

Directions What do you think it was like to live in the 1800s? Write three sentences that describe what life was like. Use a linking verb in one sentence. Use action verbs in the other two sentences.

6. _____
   _____

7. _____
   _____

8. _____
   _____

Home Activity Your child learned how to use action and linking verbs in writing. Have your child write four sentences about an event at school. Ask your child to use two action verbs and two linking verbs in the sentences.

30 Unit 2 Week 3 **Day 3**   **Grammar and Writing Practice Book**

Name _____

A Week in the 1800s

TEST PREPARATION

Action and Linking Verbs

Directions Mark the letter of the word that is an action verb.

1. Lenora added milk to the batter because it was too thick.
   A Lenora
   B looked
   C batter
   D added

2. A diligent farmer grows enough food for his whole family.
   A grows
   B enough
   C family
   D whole

3. The boy sheared the wool from the sheep.
   A sheared
   B boy
   C wool
   D sheep

4. The girls milked the cows for cheese, cream, and butter.
   A girls
   B cows
   C milked
   D for

Directions Mark the letter of the word that is a linking verb.

5. The blacksmith's shop was noisy and hot.
   A noisy
   B shop
   C and
   D was

6. We walked into the cellar, and the air smelled musty.
   A walked
   B smelled
   C into
   D musty

7. The girls feel silly in bonnets and long dresses.
   A silly
   B girls
   C feel
   D bonnets

8. Are Darlene and Mary ready for school?
   A Are
   B ready
   C school
   D for

9. Krista's chores were not easy, but she worked hard.
   A worked
   B but
   C were
   D easy

10. The cornstalks looked rough, so Jason wore gloves.
    A looked
    B wore
    C stalks
    D so

Home Activity Your child prepared for taking tests on action and linking verbs. Have your child look through a magazine or newspaper article and circle linking verbs and underline action verbs.

Grammar and Writing Practice Book Unit 2 Week 3 **Day 4** **31**

Name _____

A Week in the 1800s
CUMULATIVE REVIEW

Action and Linking Verbs

Directions Write *A* if the underlined verb is an action verb. Write *L* if the underlined verb is a linking verb. Write *PN* if the underlined word is a predicate nominative.

1. The linens <u>smelled</u> fresh.   _____
2. Who <u>mowed</u> the lawn?   _____
3. <u>Cook</u> the green beans for 15 minutes.   _____
4. I <u>am</u> tired of waking up at dawn.   _____
5. Matthew became <u>captain</u> of the team.   _____
6. Which apples <u>taste</u> sweetest?   _____
7. Emily is the best <u>cook</u>.   _____
8. The workers <u>sliced</u> the potatoes.   _____

Directions Circle *A* if the verb is an action verb. Circle *L* if it is a linking verb.

9. The boys swam in the river.   A   L
10. Nights seemed longer and darker.   A   L
11. The girls worked on their sewing.   A   L
12. The day was long and hard.   A   L
13. Father talked quietly to the horses.   A   L
14. Martha created dolls from corncobs.   A   L
15. Aunt Perley's face looked tired and pale.   A   L
16. The children played checkers before bed.   A   L
17. The pumpkin pie smells spicy.   A   L
18. Sarah feels awkward in a dress and bloomers.   A   L
19. John raced to the house.   A   L
20. They were pleased with their work.   A   L

Home Activity Your child reviewed action and linking verbs. Have your child make a chart with the headings *Action* and *Linking*, scan a page of a favorite book, and see how many action and linking verbs he or she can find to write on the chart.

Name _____

Goodbye to the Moon
DEVELOP THE CONCEPT

Subject-Verb Agreement

> The subject and verb in a sentence must **agree**, or work together. A singular subject needs a singular verb. A plural subject needs a plural verb.
>   Use the following rules for verbs that tell about the present time.
>
> - If the subject is a singular noun or *he, she,* or *it,* add *-s* or *-es* to most verbs.
>   The star *shines*. The girl *looks* at the star. She *smiles*.
> - If the subject is compound, a plural noun, or *I, you, we,* or *they*, do not add *-s* or *-es* to the verb.
>   The stars *shine*. Sarah and Renee *look* at the stars. They *smile*.
> - For the verb *be*, use *am* and *is* to agree with singular subjects and *are* to agree with plural subjects.
>   I *am* a space traveler. The astronaut *is* leaving.
>   The scientists *are* here. The pilots *are* on the plane.
> - A **collective noun** names a group, such as *family, team,* and *class*. A collective noun is singular if it refers to a group acting as one: The class *is learning* about the universe. A collective noun is plural if it refers to members of the group acting individually: The class *are disagreeing* about the size of the Milky Way.

Directions Write *Yes* if the subject and the verb in the sentence agree. If they do not agree, write *No* and the correct form of the verb.

1. The science lessons intrigues the students. _____

2. Space travelers realize the risks of lunar landings. _____

3. Passengers sometimes waits in the cramped quarters for hours. _____

4. Jordan is interested in space travel. _____

5. Her eyes is red from the smog. _____

Directions Underline the verb in ( ) that agrees with the subject.

6. Their heads (throbs, throb) from the enormous pressure.

7. Derek (are, is) ashamed of his torn jacket.

8. The stewardess (volunteers, volunteer) to get him a wheelchair.

9. Renee and Eric (marvels, marvel) at the Earth fashions.

10. The landscape (enthrall, enthralls) Sarah.

Home Activity Your child learned about subject-verb agreement. Underline several sentences in a newspaper or magazine article and ask your child to identify the subject and verb in each sentence and tell why they agree.

Grammar and Writing Practice Book

Name _____

Goodbye to the Moon

APPLY TO WRITING

Subject-Verb Agreement

Directions Write a complete sentence using the noun as the subject and the correct form of the verb.

1. teacher (explain, explains)

   _____
   _____

2. planets (rotates, rotate)

   _____
   _____

3. friends (talk, talks)

   _____
   _____

4. my cousin and I (is, are)

   _____
   _____

5. Bobby (write, writes)

   _____
   _____

6. scientists (knows, know)

   _____
   _____

7. Kepler and Ann (is, are)

   _____
   _____

8. space shuttle (soar, soars)

   _____
   _____

Home Activity Your child learned how to write subjects and verbs that agree. Have your child write three sentences about something that happened at school. Ask him or her to check that the verbs agree with the subjects.

34 Unit 2 Week 4 **Day 3**

Grammar and Writing Practice Book

Name _____

Goodbye to the Moon
TEST PREPARATION

Subject-Verb Agreement

Directions Mark the letter of the verb that agrees with the subject in each sentence.

1. Angela ___ the harness around her.
   A buckles
   B buckle's
   C buckle
   D buckling

2. The moon-dwellers ___ electrostatic filters to remove dirt.
   A use'
   B uses
   C using
   D use

3. The class ___ reading about space travel.
   A are
   B am
   C is
   D be

4. My aunt and uncle ___ for their turn.
   A waits
   B waiting
   C wait
   D wait's

5. The families ___ long weeks without sunlight.
   A enduring
   B endure
   C endures'
   D endures

6. The crewmen ___ between flights.
   A eats
   B eating
   C eat's
   D eat

7. On one visit, the kids ___ many asteroids.
   A see
   B sees
   C seen
   D see's

8. Brett ___ down the ramp to the shuttle.
   A runs
   B running
   C run
   D run's

9. Earth ___ just ahead.
   A lie
   B lies
   C lie's
   D lain

10. Bobby ___ much of his time studying planets.
    A spend
    B spend's
    C spending
    D spends

Home Activity Your child prepared for taking tests on subject-verb agreement. Ask your child to choose several of the numbered items on this page and explain to you how he or she decided which verb was correct.

Grammar and Writing Practice Book   Unit 2 Week 4 **Day 4**   **35**

Name _____

Goodbye to the Moon

CUMULATIVE REVIEW

Subject-Verb Agreement

Directions Underline the verb in ( ) that agrees with the subject.

1. The astronomers at the observatory (study, studies) the stars at night.
2. Dr. Fields (struggle, struggles) with his paperwork.
3. The Waterman family (are, is) going away for six months.
4. Both Lynn and Gene (feels, feel) cold all the time.
5. The hydroponic gardens on the moon (supply, supplies) the residents with oxygen.
6. A layer of dust and rocks (forms, form) on the floors.
7. The magnetrain (speed, speeds) over the Earth's surface.
8. The spaceships (arrives, arrive) at the destination.
9. The trip to the planets (includes, include) a wonderful view of the sun.
10. Derek and Renee (bring, brings) only two suitcases on the trip.

Directions Write a complete sentence using the correct noun as subject and the verb.

11. (airplanes, airplane) flies
    _____

12. Ben and Brad (watches, watch)
    _____

13. dogs (howls, howl)
    _____

14. stars (shine, shines)
    _____

15. two pilots (fly, flies)
    _____

Home Activity Your child reviewed subject-verb agreement. Say singular and plural subjects, such as *the house, the houses, my shoes, my shoe,* and have your child use the subjects in sentences with verbs that agree.

36 Unit 2 Week 4 **Day 5**   **Grammar and Writing Practice Book**

Name _____

Egypt

DEVELOP THE CONCEPT

Past, Present, and Future Tenses

> The **tense** of a verb shows when something happens. Verbs in the **present tense** show action that happens now. Most present tense singular verbs end with *-s*. Most present tense plural verbs do not end with *-s*.
>
> Cally <u>keeps</u> her makeup in little jars. They <u>keep</u> the makeup fresh.
>
> Verbs in the **past tense** show action that has already happened. Most verbs in the past tense end in *-ed*.
>
> She <u>brushed</u> on two coats of mascara.
>
> Verbs in the **future tense** show action that will happen. Add *will* (or *shall*) to most verbs to show the future tense.
>
> Heat <u>will make</u> mascara run.

- Some regular verbs change spelling when *-ed* is added. For verbs ending in *e*, drop the *e* and add *-ed*: *loved, hoped*. For verbs ending in a consonant and *y*, change the *y* to *i*, and add *-ed*: *cried, married*.
- For most one-syllable verbs that end in one vowel followed by one consonant, double the consonant and add *-ed*: *hopped, grabbed*.
- Irregular verbs change spelling to form the past tense: *are/were, break/broke, bring/brought, build/built, buy/bought, do/did, find/found, go/went, have/had, is/was, keep/kept, make/made, sit/sat, see/saw, take/took, teach/taught, tell/told, wear/wore, write/wrote*.

Directions Identify the tense of each underlined verb. Write *present, past,* or *future*.

1. Hieroglyphics <u>tell</u> us about ancient Egypt. _____

2. Archaeologists <u>will search</u> for artifacts. _____

3. Ramses II <u>is</u> a well-known pharaoh. _____

4. Pharaohs <u>built</u> huge statues. _____

5. Egypt <u>was</u> a major world power in 1500 B.C. _____

Directions Write the correct present, past, and future tense of each verb.

Verb	Present	Past	Future
6. find	I _____.	I _____.	I _____.
7. sit	She _____.	She _____.	She _____.
8. carry	We _____.	We _____.	We _____.

Home Activity Your child learned about past, present, and future tenses. Have your child write three sentences about Egypt using a present tense verb, a past tense verb, and a future tense verb and identifying each.

Grammar and Writing Practice Book   Unit 2 Week 5 **Day 2** **37**

Name _____

Past, Present, and Future Tenses

Directions Complete each sentence. Use a verb in the tense indicated in ( ).

1. (present) Like the Egyptians, we _____

2. (present) Students will leave for the museum as soon as _____

3. (future) Before Mike delivers his report on mummies, _____

4. (past) Thousands of years ago, _____

5. (future) Before the semester is over, _____

6. (past) Women in Egypt _____

7. (present) Head coverings _____

8. (future) Because Sally wants to get an A in history, _____

Directions What do you think life in ancient Egypt was for kids your age? Use past tense verbs in your sentences.

_____
_____
_____
_____
_____

Home Activity Your child learned how to use past, present, and future tenses in writing. Have your child write about things he or she did yesterday, does today, and will do tomorrow. Ask your child to explain the verb tense he or she used in each sentence.

Name _____

Egypt
TEST PREPARATION

Past, Present, and Future Tenses

Directions Mark the letter of the verb that correctly completes each sentence.

1. Thousands of years ago, ancient Egyptians _____ songs about love.
   A write
   B wrote
   C are writing
   D will write

2. I like Mr. Parkinson because he _____ his students after class.
   A helps
   B was helped
   C will helped'
   D will helping

3. From now on, Marlie _____ her history homework after class.
   A does
   B doing
   C will do
   D did

4. Last week, Connie _____ a statue of Nefertiti at the museum gift shop.
   A buys
   B bought
   C is buying
   D will buy

Directions Mark the letter of the past tense form of the underlined verb.

5. Upper-class women <u>wear</u> jewelry with gold and precious gems.
   A weared
   B were wore
   C wore
   D will wear

6. In most homes, bread <u>is</u> a basic food.
   A am
   B are
   C were
   D was

7. Pharaohs <u>collect</u> food from the farmers as taxes.
   A will collect
   B collected
   C are collecting
   D will be collecting

8. Women <u>keep</u> their makeup in tiny bowls.
   A kept
   B will keep
   C keeped
   D were keep

Home Activity Your child prepared for taking tests on past, present, and future tenses. List *take*, *make*, *build*, and *are* on paper. Have your child write the past and future tenses for each verb.

Grammar and Writing Practice Book Unit 2 Week 5 **Day 4** **39**

Name _____

Egypt
CUMULATIVE REVIEW

Past, Present, and Future Tenses

Directions Identify the tense of each underlined verb. Write *present*, *past*, or *future*.

1. Egypt <u>is</u> in Africa. _____

2. Pharaohs <u>lived</u> in luxury. _____

3. The Moore family <u>will visit</u> Egypt. _____

4. They <u>will find</u> other Egyptian artifacts. _____

5. Thirty-one dynasties <u>reigned</u> in Egypt. _____

6. Memphis, Thebes, and Cairo <u>were</u> capitals of Egypt. _____

7. The Great Pyramid <u>covers</u> thirteen acres. _____

8. Some blocks in the Great Pyramid <u>weigh</u> fifteen tons. _____

Directions Rewrite each sentence twice. First, change the underlined verb to past tense. Then change it to future tense.

9. Burial chambers <u>tell</u> us about ancient Egypt.

   Past: _____

   Future: _____

10. Egyptians <u>carry</u> possessions to the chambers.

    Past: _____

    Future: _____

11. They <u>use</u> a stone coffin called a sarcophagus.

    Past: _____

    Future: _____

12. Archaeologists <u>find</u> burial chambers in other cultures.

    Past: _____

    Future: _____

Home Activity Your child reviewed past, present, and future tenses. Ask your child to look through a magazine article and find examples of past, present, and future tense verbs.

40 Unit 2 Week 5 **Day 5**   **Grammar and Writing Practice Book**

Name _____

Hatchet

DEVELOP THE CONCEPT

Principal Parts of Regular Verbs

> A verb's tenses are made from four basic forms. These basic forms are called the verb's **principal parts.**
>
> | **Present** | **Present Participle** | **Past** | **Past Participle** |
> |---|---|---|---|
> | watch | (am, is, are) watching | watched | (has, have, had) watched |
> | carry | (am, is, are) carrying | carried | (has, have, had) carried |
>
> A **regular verb** forms its past and past participle by adding *-ed* or *-d* to the present form.
> - The present and the past form can be used by themselves as verbs.
> - The present participle and the past participle are always used with a helping verb.
>
> Remember, when a verb ends with a consonant and *y*, change the *y* to *i* before adding *-ed*: *cried*. When a one-syllable verb ends with a vowel and a consonant, double the consonant before adding *-ed*: *hopped*.

Directions Write *present, present participle, past,* or *past participle* to identify the principal part of the underlined verb.

1. The bobcat limped away into the trees. _____
2. Sparks from the rock are raining down on the cave floor. _____
3. She places more wood on the fire. _____
4. The darkness has filled him with fear. _____
5. He scrapes bark from the tree with his hatchet. _____
6. The plane slammed into the forest. _____
7. Mosquitoes are swarming around Brian's head. _____

Directions Underline the verb in each sentence. Write *present, present participle, past,* or *past participle* to identify the principal part used to form the verb.

8. Alex is hiking along the path with his two brothers. _____
9. His grandfather owned a twin engine plane. _____
10. Steve and Mike are wiping the grease from the engine. _____
11. The snakes have slithered away from the fire. _____
12. Jane picks the roots from the ground. _____

Home Activity Your child learned about principal parts of regular verbs. Have your child describe activities in your home using present participle forms of verbs: *My sisters are playing outside. Mom is reading the mail.*

Grammar and Writing Practice Book Unit 3 Week 1 **Day 2** **41**

Name _____

Hatchet

APPLY TO WRITING

Principal Parts of Regular Verbs

Directions Write a sentence using the principal part of the verb as indicated in ( ).

1. learn (present participle with *is*)
   _____
   _____

2. listen (past)
   _____
   _____

3. learn (present)
   _____
   _____

4. stop (past participle with *had*)
   _____
   _____

5. guard (present participle with *are*)
   _____
   _____

6. burn (past participle with *have*)
   _____
   _____

7. ask (past)
   _____
   _____

8. grasp (present)
   _____
   _____

Home Activity Your child learned how to use principal parts of regular verbs in writing. Have your child write four sentences about his or her favorite movie. Each sentence should use a different principal part of the verb *watch*.

Name _____

Hatchet
TEST PREPARATION

Principal Parts of Regular Verbs

Directions Mark the letter that indicates the correct form of the underlined verb.

1. The forest rangers <u>are advancing</u> through the dense fog.
   A Present
   B Present participle
   C Past
   D Past participle

2. The stone <u>skipped</u> across the smooth surface of the lake.
   A Present
   B Present participle
   C Past
   D Past participle

3. Shelly <u>is swatting</u> at the mosquitoes with a tree branch.
   A Present
   B Present participle
   C Past
   D Past participle

4. Maryann <u>crawls</u> slowly away from the skunk.
   A Present
   B Present participle
   C Past
   D Past participle

5. From the plane, Brian <u>had watched</u> the trees grow closer.
   A Present
   B Present participle
   C Past
   D Past participle

6. The hikers <u>had examined</u> the map before breakfast.
   A Present
   B Present participle
   C Past
   D Past participle

7. Faye <u>is considering</u> a trip to the Northwest Territories.
   A Present
   B Present participle
   C Past
   D Past participle

8. Marc <u>leaned</u> against the cold, damp cave wall.
   A Present
   B Present participle
   C Past
   D Past participle

9. Jake <u>approaches</u> the dark cave.
   A Present
   B Present participle
   C Past
   D Past participle

10. Kris <u>scaled</u> the side of the cliff.
    A Present
    B Present participle
    C Past
    D Past participle

Home Activity Your child prepared for taking tests on principal parts of regular verbs. Ask your child to write four regular verbs that tell about things he or she can do (*play, kick, skate, dance*) and then write the four principal parts for each verb.

Grammar and Writing Practice Book Unit 3 Week 1 Day 4 **43**

Principal Parts of Regular Verbs

Directions Write *present*, *present participle*, *past*, or *past participle* to identify the principal part of the underlined verb.

1. The children are picking wild strawberries. _____
2. The shelter protects Rosa from the rain. _____
3. Dan sharpened his hatchet with a file. _____
4. Carrie had hoped the matches were dry. _____
5. The sun is moving toward the west. _____
6. Jenny waves to us from the plane. _____
7. Brian wondered if he would ever be found. _____
8. Tara jumped every time she heard a noise. _____
9. Bobby had covered the radio with a tarp. _____
10. Jake ripped the paper into shreds. _____

Directions Complete each sentence with the principal part of the given verb as indicated in ( ).

11. Hungry and tired, Will _____ the root from the ground. (pull/past tense)
12. Chelsea and Ron _____ the batteries in the flashlight before they set out. (change/past participle with *had*)
13. Kira _____ strips of bark and small twigs. (gather/present participle with *is*)
14. She _____ the bark from the trees. (peel/present)
15. The rescuers did not know how much Brian _____. (suffer/past participle with *had*)

Name _____

When Marian Sang
DEVELOP THE CONCEPT

Principal Parts of Irregular Verbs

Usually you add *-ed* to a verb to form the past and past participle. **Irregular verbs** do not follow this rule. Instead of having *-ed* forms, irregular verbs usually change to other words.

Present Tense	Benny writes a pop song.
Present Participle	He is writing a pop song.
Past Tense	Benny wrote several pop songs.
Past Participle	He has written pop songs for several years.

Present Tense	Present Participle	Past Tense	Past Participle
begin	(am, is, are) beginning	began	(has, have, had) begun
bring	(am, is, are) bringing	brought	(has, have, had) brought
buy	(am, is, are) buying	bought	(has, have, had) bought
come	(am, is, are) coming	came	(has, have, had) come
feel	(am, is, are) feeling	felt	(has, have, had) felt
grow	(am, is, are) growing	grew	(has, have, had) grown
keep	(am, is, are) keeping	kept	(has, have, had) kept
see	(am, is, are) seeing	saw	(has, have, had) seen
take	(am, is, are) taking	took	(has, have, had) taken
tell	(am, is, are) telling	told	(has, have, had) told
write	(am, is, are) writing	wrote	(has, have, had) written

Directions Write *present, present participle, past,* or *past participle* to identify the principal part used to form the underlined verb.

1. Marian began music school at eighteen. _____

2. Her family had come to Europe for her concert. _____

3. Joe is beginning his singing career. _____

4. Jenny keeps a glass of water nearby. _____

Directions Underline the form of the verb in ( ) that correctly completes each sentence.

5. Dana (feeled, felt) faint after singing in the warm hall.

6. Tom (had written, writed) a letter to his favorite folk singer.

7. Charlie (buyed, bought) a ticket and went to the musical.

8. Cathy (has began, began) her voice lessons.

 Home Activity Your child learned about principal parts of irregular verbs. Together look through a newspaper or magazine. Have your child find three irregular verbs and identify which principal part of each verb is being used.

Grammar and Writing Practice Book   Unit 3 Week 2 **Day 2** **45**

Name _____

When Marian Sang

APPLY TO WRITING

Principal Parts of Irregular Verbs

Directions Write a sentence using the principal part of the given verb as indicated in ( ).

1. see (past tense)
_____

2. feel (present participle with *is*)
_____

3. take (past participle with *had*)
_____

4. bring (present)
_____

5. become (present participle with *are*)
_____

6. choose (past participle with *had*)
_____

7. leave (past)
_____

8. know (present)
_____

9. sing (present participle with *is*)
_____

10. tell (past)
_____

Home Activity Your child learned how to use principal parts of irregular verbs in writing. Have your child write three sentences about an adventure with a friend using three different irregular verbs in the past tense.

46 Unit 3 Week 2 **Day 3** **Grammar and Writing Practice Book**

Name _____

When Marian Sang

TEST PREPARATION

Principal Parts of Irregular Verbs

Directions Mark the letter of the verb that correctly completes each sentence.

1. The orchestra _____ a break.
   A took
   B taked
   C taking
   D has took

2. Prejudice _____ Marian from living her dream.
   A keeping
   B is keep
   C kept
   D keeped

3. Tessa _____ into a talented young alto.
   A grown
   B had grown
   C growed
   D growing

4. Mr. Boghetti _____ her Italian songs.
   A gives
   B had give
   C gaves
   D gaved

5. Michael _____ with the Metropolitan Opera.
   A has sang
   B singing
   C sanged
   D is singing

6. They _____ that the trolley would not stop.
   A known
   B knew
   C is knowed
   D knowed

7. Viola _____ New York for Paris.
   A leaving
   B leaved
   C is leaving
   D is leaved

8. She _____ about the beauty of the concert hall.
   A hearing
   B had heard
   C heared
   D is heared

9. Sherry _____ her concert ticket away.
   A had given
   B had gave
   C gived
   D are give

10. He _____ his understudy for the role.
    A choosing
    B have chosed
    C chose
    D choosed

Home Activity Your child prepared for taking tests on principal parts of irregular verbs. Help your child make flash cards for the principal parts of difficult irregular verbs, such as *sing*, *take*, *bring*, and *know*, by writing the present form on one side and the other forms on the other side. Quiz your child with the cards.

Grammar and Writing Practice Book Unit 3 Week 2 Day 4 **47**

Name _____

When Marian Sang

CUMULATIVE REVIEW

Principal Parts of Irregular Verbs

Directions Write *present, present participle, past,* or *past participle* to identify the principal part used to form the underlined verb.

1. Marian <u>felt</u> nervous in front of the audience of 75,000 people. _____
2. Mrs. Anderson <u>feels</u> proud of her daughter. _____
3. Esther <u>is beginning</u> a new role. _____
4. She often <u>sings</u> with her eyes closed. _____
5. The quartet <u>had chosen</u> an old Civil War song. _____
6. Marian <u>told</u> about her love of singing. _____
7. She <u>has taken</u> her pain and turned it into beautiful music. _____

Directions Underline the form of the verb in ( ) that correctly completes each sentence.

8. Mother and Father (are speaking, have spoke) with Mr. Boghetti about Marian's future.
9. She (had become, had became) a symbol for her people.
10. Fans (writing, wrote) letters protesting the sponsor's decision.
11. The Russian audience (gave, gived) the opera singer a standing ovation.
12. Kelsey (has keeped, keeps) in touch with her mother in America.
13. People all over the world (heard/is hearing) Marian sing.
14. Marian (had sang/sang) in many different countries.
15. She (knowed/had known) she would sing in Russia.

Home Activity Your child reviewed principal parts of irregular verbs. Have your child listen to a dialogue between two people and write some irregular verbs that are used. Have your child use the list to make a chart and fill in the other principal parts of each verb.

48 Unit 3 Week 2 Day 5

Grammar and Writing Practice Book

Name _____

Learning to Swim

DEVELOP THE CONCEPT

Verbs, Objects, and Subject Complements

> A **direct object** follows an action verb and tells who or what receives the action of the verb.
>   Meg gave a signal. (*Gave* is an action verb. *Signal* is a direct object.)
>
> An **indirect object** follows an action verb and tells to whom or what the action of the verb is done.
>   Meg gave Luis a signal. (The indirect object *Luis* tells to whom Meg gave a signal. Note that an indirect object comes before the direct object.)
>
> A **subject complement** follows a linking verb and tells who or what the subject is or is like.
>   Chidi seemed sad. (*Seemed* is a linking verb and *sad* is a subject complement that describes Chidi.)
>   Todd is the captain of the team. (*Is* is a linking verb, and *captain* is a subject complement telling who Todd is.)
>
> • A noun used as a subject complement is a predicate noun. An adjective used as a subject complement is a predicate adjective.

Directions Write the subject complement in each sentence.

1. The waves seemed rough. _____

2. The flutter kick is a strong kick used with the crawl. _____

3. The water felt cool in the July sun. _____

4. Ice cream tastes refreshing on a hot day at the beach. _____

5. Jill was happy about her progress. _____

Directions Circle direct objects and underline any indirect objects.

6. Ted visited his grandparents' village.

7. Barb handed Dex a dry towel.

8. Adam prefers soccer to aquatic sports.

9. My mother taught me rules for safe swimming.

10. Sylvia set a new record for her team.

11. Sandy gave her sisters matching blue swimsuits.

12. Anne practiced the breaststroke.

Home Activity Your child learned about verbs, objects, and subject complements. Have your child tell you what direct objects, indirect objects, and subject complements are and find two examples of each in the newspaper.

Grammar and Writing Practice Book

Name _____

Learning to Swim

APPLY TO WRITING

Verbs, Objects, and Subject Complements

Directions Add a direct object to complete each sentence.

1. Swimmers practice _____ so they can swim the length of the pool.
2. Aunt Jane took a _____ to the ocean.
3. Dad clapped his _____ when he saw how far we swam.
4. I won the _____ at school.
5. Gwen waved her _____ to signal for help.

Directions Add an indirect object to complete each sentence.

6. Uncle Jim taught his _____ the dog paddle.
7. Bette gave a _____ directions to the beach.
8. Cheryl taught _____ the backstroke.
9. Show your _____ the changing room.
10. I gave my _____ earplugs.

Directions Write three sentences about swimming. Use at least one indirect object, one direct object, and one subject complement in your sentences.

_____
_____
_____
_____
_____
_____
_____
_____
_____
_____

Home Activity Your child learned how to use verbs, objects, and subject complements in writing. Ask your child to write a paragraph about a favorite sport. Have your child use objects and subject complements in his or her writing.

Name _____

Learning to Swim
TEST PREPARATION

Verbs, Objects, and Subject Complements

Directions Mark the letter of the sentence that has a subject complement.

1. A Mindy's arms felt sore as she swam to shore.
   B The kids swam all the way to the dock.
   C The girls ran as fast as they could.
   D The dog paddle helps children learn to swim.

2. A You might not enjoy swimming lessons.
   B Tim grew tired and started to tread water.
   C Breathe when your head is out of the water.
   D In Linda's first swimming lesson, she floated.

3. A The peppermint ice cream tasted good.
   B A fisherman drowned in a rip tide.
   C The stranger wore shorts and a T-shirt.
   D Judy practiced swimming lengths of the pool.

4. A Sunbathers crowded the beach.
   B The mother said encouraging words to her daughter.
   C She forgot her towels.
   D Swimming is a popular sport.

Directions Mark the letter of the direct object of the underlined verb in the sentence.

5. Emma won the contest by swimming faster than anyone else.
   A won   C anyone else
   B contest   D swimming faster

6. David touched the wall and turned to swim back.
   A turned   C pool
   B back   D wall

7. Carly drew diagrams in the sand with a stick.
   A sand   C diagrams
   B drew   D stick

8. Erik took a test to determine how far he could swim.
   A determine   C how far
   B test   D swim

Home Activity Your child prepared for taking tests on verbs, objects, and subject complements. Read a favorite story with your child. Ask him or her to find direct objects, indirect objects, and subject complements in the story.

Grammar and Writing Practice Book   Unit 3 Week 3 **Day 4** **51**

Name _____

Learning to Swim

CUMULATIVE REVIEW

Verbs, Objects, and Subject Complements

Directions Write the subject complement in each sentence.

1. The sea air smelled clean. _____
2. Larry is a strong swimmer. _____
3. Max was calm in the strong current. _____
4. The girls looked sad when they lost the race. _____
5. Laura became a good swimming teacher. _____

Directions Circle direct objects and underline any indirect objects.

6. Paul bent his knees so he could kick.
7. Mother told me a story about the ocean.
8. The Festival of Stars celebrates a meeting between two characters.
9. Write your wishes on colored paper.
10. The teacher offered Cindy some tips about breathing.
11. She added distance by weaving back and forth in the water.
12. Waves pounded the shore at high tide.
13. Show her the stroke so she can see what to do.
14. Dan won a gold medal in the Olympics.
15. I showed my gym teacher my frog kick.
16. I asked her questions about the Olympic winners.
17. Mira gave me articles from an old newspaper.
18. I have set goals for the future.

Home Activity Your child reviewed verbs, objects, and subject complements. Have your child look through a magazine and find three subject complements and three direct objects.

52 Unit 3 Week 3 **Day 5** **Grammar and Writing Practice Book**

Name _____

Juan Verdades

DEVELOP THE CONCEPT

Troublesome Verbs

Some pairs of verbs are **troublesome verbs** because they look alike or have similar meanings.

Verb	Meaning	Present	Past	Past Participle
sit	sit down	sit	sat	(has, have, had) sat
set	put or place	set	set	(has, have, had) set
lie	rest or recline	lie	lay	(has, have, had) lain
lay	put or place	lay	laid	(has, have, had) laid
rise	get or move up	rise	rose	(has, have, had) risen
raise	lift something up	raise	raised	(has, have, had) raised
let	allow or permit	let	let	(has, have, had) let
leave	go away	leave	left	(has, have, had) left
lend	give to someone	lend	lent	(has, have, had) lent
borrow	get from someone	borrow	borrowed	(has, have, had) borrowed
teach	show how	teach	taught	(has, have, had) taught
learn	find out	learn	learned	(has, have, had) learned

Directions Underline the correct verb in each sentence.

1. She had (raised, risen) the window in the kitchen.

2. Don Arturo has (laid, lain) awake many nights.

3. Araceli (taught, learned) her friend Juan a good lesson.

4. (Sit, Set) the silverware on the table.

5. The wealthy rancheros have (sat, set) in the village plaza.

Directions Complete each sentence with the correct verb from the list above.

6. Will you _____ me some money until next Tuesday?

7. Yesterday, Juan _____ his house and went to the fields.

8. The men in the village _____ from their chairs when it was time to go home.

9. Yesterday, Ms. Cortez _____ us the Spanish word for *apple*.

10. _____ me go out to the orchard to pick fruit from the trees.

Home Activity Your child learned about troublesome verbs. Have your child choose pairs of verbs from the list on this page, use them correctly in sentences, and explain how he or she knew which verb to use.

Name _____

Juan Verdades
APPLY TO WRITING

Troublesome Verbs

Directions Choose the verb in ( ) that correctly completes each sentence. Write the verb.

1. The ranchers _____ the foremen run the ranches. (leave, let)

2. Yesterday, the wealthy landowners _____ colorful blankets on the ground and sat down. (laid, lay)

3. Raul _____ him about honesty. (learned, taught)

4. Don Ignacio _____ his finger and shook it at his friend. (raised, rose)

5. When Araceli marries Juan, she will wear a veil that she _____ from her cousin. (borrowed, lent)

6. The workers have _____ their baskets down. (set, sit)

7. Señora Arturo _____ down for a nap in the afternoon. (lies, lays)

8. When floodwaters _____, the family piles sandbags outside the house. (raise, rise)

Directions Write a paragraph describing a family dinner. Begin with preparing the table. Use as many principal parts of *set, sit, lie, lay, leave, let, rise,* and *raise* as you can.

_____

_____

_____

_____

_____

_____

_____

_____

_____

_____

Home Activity Your child learned how to use troublesome verbs in writing. Have your child select pairs of troublesome verbs and demonstrate how to use the verbs correctly by writing two sentences with one of the verbs in each sentence.

54 Unit 3 Week 4 **Day 3**   **Grammar and Writing Practice Book**

Name _____

Juan Verdades
TEST PREPARATION

Troublesome Verbs

Directions Mark the letter of the verb that correctly completes each sentence.

1. The girls _____ a ladder against the tree so they could pick apples.
   A sat
   B set
   C have sat
   D setted

2. When the sun came out, the workers _____ their coats on the ground.
   A will lie
   B lied
   C laid
   D lain

3. Araceli _____ her father a lesson about truthfulness.
   A teached
   B learns
   C learned
   D taught

4. The rancher _____ quietly so Juan could think about his response.
   A let
   B left
   C leaved
   D have let

Directions Mark the letter of the sentence that has the correct verb.

5. A Maria sits in a rocking chair on the porch of the hacienda.
   B Juan sat the basket of apples in the house.
   C Araceli's father lays down to rest.
   D Don Arturo left his friend talk him into making a bet.

6. A When the sun raises overhead, it is time for lunch.
   B Carmen lies her books on the chair.
   C Leanna lays her backpack on the bench.
   D Marguerite borrowed her white shoes to Araceli.

7. A Folk stories often lie down a lesson.
   B The sun rises in the east.
   C The rancher lies his keys on his desk.
   D Juan lent a ladder from the shed.

8. A Don Arturo learned an important lesson about trust.
   B Juan learned his boss an important lesson.
   C When the sun sat in the west, the workers went home.
   D Please leave me go to the wedding.

Home Activity Your child prepared for taking tests on troublesome verbs. Ask your child to look through a newspaper article and find three sentences in which troublesome verbs are used correctly.

Grammar and Writing Practice Book

Name _____

Juan Verdades
CUMULATIVE REVIEW

Troublesome Verbs

Directions Write the letter of the definition of the underlined verb.

_____ 1. Juan <u>left</u> the orchard.   A gave

_____ 2. <u>Set</u> the basket on the ground.   B lifted up

_____ 3. He <u>raised</u> his arms and stretched. C was seated

_____ 4. She <u>lent</u> a dress to her cousin.   D went away from

_____ 5. Teresa <u>sat</u> on the lawn.   E place or put

Directions Write the form of the underlined verb indicated in ( ).

6. Juan and Araceli <u>sit</u> together at the table and drank coffee. (past) _____

7. The men had <u>rise</u> to their feet and saluted the flag. (past participle) _____

8. The girls <u>lie</u> in lawn chairs near the orchard. (present) _____

9. Don Ignatio <u>let</u> Juan have the ranch because he told the truth. (past) _____

10. The gardener has <u>set</u> out tulip bulbs. (past participle) _____

Directions Underline the correct verb in each sentence.

11. He had (laid, lain) the tools on the sidewalk.

12. Señora Arturo (borrowed, lent) a needle and thread from her hostess.

13. Don't (lend, borrow) your valuable belongings to anyone.

14. Juan (taught, learned) his children an important lesson.

15. The workers (taught, learned) how to speak English.

Home Activity Your child reviewed troublesome verbs. Have your child write several sentences about what he or she does in the morning using at least three troublesome verbs.

Name _____

Elizabeth Blackwell

DEVELOP THE CONCEPT

Prepositions

A **preposition** shows a relationship between a noun or pronoun and another word in the sentence, such as a verb, adjective, or other noun. A **prepositional phrase** begins with a **preposition** and usually ends with a noun or pronoun. The noun or pronoun is called the **object of the preposition.**

Luke lived above the pharmacy. ← Prepositional Phrase

Preposition   Object of the Preposition

Here are some prepositions: *about, above, across, after, against, along, among, around, as, at, before, behind, below, beneath, beside, between, beyond, by, down, during, except, for, from, in, inside, into, near, of, off, on, onto, out, outside, over, past, since, through, throughout, to, toward, under, underneath, until, up, upon, with, within, without.*

- Like an adjective, a prepositional phrase can modify a noun or pronoun.
  She wrote to her brother at medical school.
- Like an adverb, a prepositional phrase can modify a verb.
  An angry crowd gathered outside the clinic.

Directions Circle the preposition and underline the object of the preposition in each prepositional phrase.

1. She could barely see her patient in the dim light.

2. Stephanie had questions about the anatomy lesson.

3. The infection formed inside the baby's eyes.

4. Sadly, one of the patients died.

5. The angry mob rushed toward the lady doctor's home.

Directions Underline the prepositional phrase in each sentence. Write *Adjective* if the prepositional phrase acts as an adjective. Write *Adverb* if it acts as an adverb.

6. Brandon and Tracey studied outside the medical building.   _____

7. Zak sat beneath the shady tree.   _____

8. Elizabeth Blackwell paved a road for other women.   _____

9. Dr. Blot is a graduate of St. Bartholomew's Medical College.   _____

Home Activity Your child learned about prepositions. Have your child scan a paragraph from a newspaper article and underline each preposition and circle each object of the preposition.

Grammar and Writing Practice Book   Unit 3 Week 5 **Day 2** 57

Name _____

Elizabeth Blackwell

APPLY TO WRITING

Prepositions

Directions Add a prepositional phrase to each sentence. Write the new sentence.

1. The injured man hobbled.
_____

2. His sister waved.
_____

3. The ambulance raced.
_____

4. April studied medicine.
_____

5. I spoke to Dr. Lynn.
_____

6. The hospital director is away.
_____

7. Alex had never gone.
_____

8. My friend and I hurried.
_____

9. Can you help me walk?
_____

10. The mother cried.
_____

Home Activity Your child learned how to use prepositions in writing. Have your child write sentences describing the locations of objects in the room using at least one prepositional phrase in each sentence.

Name _____

Elizabeth Blackwell
TEST PREPARATION

Prepositions

Directions Mark the letter of the prepositions in each sentence.

1. The clinic is located down the street and around the corner.
   A down, and
   B located, around
   C down, around
   D street, corner

2. Jeff stayed in the hospital for three days.
   A in, for
   B the, three
   C in, three
   D hospital, days

3. By the morning, she could not see across the room.
   A morning, room
   B By, across
   C not, across
   D by, the

4. Dr. Blot removed the film from the pupil of her eye.
   A the, her
   B film, pupil
   C pupil, eye
   D from, of

Directions Mark the letter of the objects of the prepositions in each sentence.

5. He placed the scalpel on the tray beside the forceps.
   A placed, beside
   B scalpel, tray, forceps
   C tray, forceps
   D on, beside

6. After her experience at St. Bartholomew's, Elizabeth returned home.
   A After, at
   B experience, St. Bartholomew's
   C St. Bartholomew's, Elizabeth
   D experience, Elizabeth

7. She carefully walked up the stairs with the sick child.
   A stairs, child
   B she, stairs
   C up, sick
   D up, with

8. Immigrants within the neighborhood were shocked by her recommendations.
   A Immigrants, recommendations
   B in, by
   C Immigrants, neighborhood
   D neighborhood, recommendations

Home Activity Your child prepared for taking tests on prepositions. Read aloud sentences from a favorite book. Pause after each sentence and ask your child to identify any prepositional phrases in the sentence.

Grammar and Writing Practice Book   Unit 3 Week 5 **Day 4**

Name _____

Elizabeth Blackwell
CUMULATIVE REVIEW

Prepositions

Directions Circle the preposition and underline the object of the preposition in each prepositional phrase.

1. Dr. Miller drew the medicine into the syringe.
2. She stood over the crib and examined the baby.
3. The nurse on the tenth floor caught the baby's disease.
4. Dr. Phillips took a nap between surgeries.
5. She took a deep breath and stepped inside the operating room.
6. Dr. Blackwell saved my son from cholera.
7. Mr. Freeman was scheduled for surgery after the first of the year.
8. An alarm sounded at the nurse's station on the seventh floor.

Directions Underline the prepositional phrase in each sentence. Write *Adjective* if the prepositional phrase acts as an adjective. Write *Adverb* if it acts as an adverb.

9. All the doctors in the room were assisting Dr. Blackwell. _____
10. The nurse always worries when the temperature drops below zero. _____
11. Our sixth-grade class took a field trip to the medical center. _____
12. They built a new hospital for disabled veterans. _____

Directions Add a prepositional phrase to each sentence. Write the new sentence.

13. We saw the doctor walk.

_____

14. I followed my teacher.

_____

15. Can you run?

_____

Home Activity Your child reviewed prepositions. Have your child create a way to remember prepositions. *The plane flies* **through** *the cloud,* **around** *the cloud,* **near** *the cloud,* **below** *the cloud,* **into** *the cloud,* **under** *the cloud,* etc.

60 Unit 3 Week 5 **Day 5** **Grammar and Writing Practice Book**

Subject and Object Pronouns

A personal pronoun used as the subject of a sentence is called a **subject pronoun**.
She planned an archaeological dig. He and I heard the details.

A personal pronoun used as a direct object, indirect object, or object of a preposition is called an **object pronoun**.
The sea captain took us for a ride. He told him and me stories.

- Subject pronouns are *I, you, he, she, it, we,* and *they*.
- Object pronouns are *me, you, him, her, it, us,* and *them*.
- Remember to use the correct pronoun form with a compound subject or object pronoun.
- Subject pronouns replace the nouns they represent. Do not use a subject pronoun with the noun it represents.
    No: Carrie she studied oceanography.
    Yes: Carrie studied oceanography.

Directions Circle the pronoun in ( ) that completes each sentence correctly.

1. (I, Me) am fascinated by maritime exploration.
2. (Them, They) believed the sea captain was a good navigator.
3. Robert and (he, him) read about the first people to reach the North Pole.
4. (We, Us) studied relics and artifacts.
5. Bill and (me, I) studied the habitat of the penguin.
6. David and (she, her) have always wanted to visit Alaska.
7. Mr. Douglas taught me and (her, she) about Arctic explorers.
8. The class put the fossils back in the case after students studied (they, them).
9. Teddy Roosevelt supported Admiral Peary and often wrote to (he, him).
10. She took (us, we) on a field trip.
11. I helped Sara and (they, them) with the science project.
12. My sister told you and (me, I) stories about her visit to Alaska.

Home Activity Your child learned about subject and object pronouns. Have your child show you subject and object pronouns in something he or she has written.

Name _____

Into the Ice

APPLY TO WRITING

Subject and Object Pronouns

Directions Write the pronoun in ( ) that completes each sentence correctly.

1. My friends and (I, me) dream about adventures. _____

2. A trip to the desert seems exciting to Sheila and (he, him). _____

3. You and (she, her) should hike in the Rocky Mountains. _____

4. I told Jorge and (they, them) about the whitewater raft trip. _____

5. A bike trip would be perfect for my parents and (I, me). _____

6. Leon asked Jill and (she, her) if they had been to Mexico. _____

7. Bob and (he, him) followed the guide up the trail. _____

8. Paula and (they, them) took the boat to the islands. _____

Directions Write a paragraph about an exploration, adventure, or discovery you would like to try with a friend. Be sure to use compound subject and object pronouns correctly.

_____
_____
_____
_____
_____
_____
_____
_____
_____
_____
_____

Home Activity Your child learned how to use subject and object pronouns in writing. Ask your child to write about somewhere he or she went with friends. Ask your child to use at least one subject pronoun and one object pronoun.

62 Unit 4 Week 1 **Day 3**

Grammar and Writing Practice Book

Subject and Object Pronouns

Directions Mark the letter of the pronoun that correctly replaces the underlined word or words in each sentence.

1. Admiral Peary and Dr. Cook wanted to reach the North Pole first.
   A They
   B Us
   C Them
   D We

2. The Inuit called Marie Peary a blond snowbaby.
   A you
   B she
   C her
   D it

3. The sledges could glide over the ice pack.
   A him
   B it
   C they
   D them

4. Admiral Peary thanked the Inuit for their help.
   A it
   B they
   C them
   D us

5. A woman loaded furs, and then the woman prepared dinner.
   A him
   B them
   C her
   D she

6. Mother asked Pat and me to turn the volume down.
   A us
   B we
   C they
   D she

7. Robert Peary was brave. Robert Peary was also arrogant.
   A Him
   B He
   C Her
   D Them

8. Dr. Cook did not think Peary would get there before Dr. Cook.
   A she
   B they
   C he
   D him

9. The dogs were among the best dogs the Inuit had.
   A Us
   B They
   C Him
   D Her

10. The explorers longed to reach the Pole.
    A They
    B Us
    C Her
    D Them

Home Activity Your child prepared for taking tests on subject and object pronouns. With your child, read a magazine article. Have your child circle subject pronouns and underline object pronouns on one page in the article.

Subject and Object Pronouns

Directions Circle the pronoun in each sentence. Write *SP* if it is a subject pronoun and *OP* if it is an object pronoun.

1. We felt bad that Admiral Peary's claims were disputed. _____

2. The snow skis were bought for Ronny and me. _____

3. Josephine Peary told them about the Arctic. _____

4. He and the men hoped to reach the North Pole first. _____

5. At last they spotted a ship on the horizon. _____

Directions Circle the pronoun in ( ) that completes each sentence correctly.

6. Anna and (he, him) needed to do more research on Admiral Peary.

7. (They, Them) listed the obstacles an Arctic explorer might encounter.

8. (She, Her) was one of the few women who went on expeditions.

9. (We, Us) believe Admiral Peary was a great explorer.

10. Charles and (I, me) looked for a biography of Dr. Frederick A. Cook.

11. Peary quarreled with Cook and refused to allow (he, him) to publish a paper.

12. The curator gave Michael and (she, her) records on Peary's travels.

13. The compass pointed (he, him) in the right direction.

14. The tour was taken by Mr. Blades and (we, us).

15. My teacher gave Stacey and (I, me) an A on our Arctic Circle report.

Home Activity Your child reviewed subject and object pronouns. Ask your child to use subject and object pronouns in a letter he or she writes to a friend or family member.

Name _____

The Chimpanzees I Love
DEVELOP THE CONCEPT

Pronouns and Antecedents

> A **pronoun** takes the place of a noun or nouns. An **antecedent**, or referent, is the noun or nouns to which the pronoun refers. A pronoun and its antecedent must agree in number and gender.
>
> Before you use a pronoun, ask yourself whether the antecedent is singular or plural. If the antecedent is singular, decide whether it is masculine, feminine, or neuter. Then choose a pronoun that agrees. In the following sentences, the antecedents are underlined once; the pronouns are underlined twice.
>
> Jay and I walked to the zoo, and we saw the new exhibit.
> Jay called Carla to pick him up from the zoo.

Directions Circle the pronoun that refers to the underlined antecedent.

1. Infant chimps are cute and cuddly, but eventually (they, it) become more difficult.
2. Faustino's mother tried to comfort (him, them).
3. (We, They) humans must learn to respect the animal kingdom.
4. The African forest is perfect for chimps because (they, it) is full of life.
5. The chimp was caught in a snare, but (he, you) was able to break free.
6. I convinced Tim that (it, he) should come to the zoo with me.
7. Jane Goodall worked at the Gombe Stream Research Center, where (she, they) studied chimps.
8. Chimps sometimes make a tool and use (them, it).

Directions Write the pronoun that completes each sentence. Underline the antecedent to which the pronoun refers.

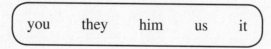

you   they   him   us   it

9. Hunters kill the animals so _____ can sell the meat in the big town.
10. The "bush-meat trade" will be hard to stop because _____ is a big money-making operation.
11. Dr. John wanted JoJo to walk to _____.
12. Alexander and I sat next to Fax, and she played with _____.

Home Activity Your child learned about pronouns and antecedents. Have your child find examples of singular or plural antecedents in a favorite book.

Grammar and Writing Practice Book   Unit 4 Week 2 **Day 2** **65**

Name _____

The Chimpanzees I Love

APPLY TO WRITING

Pronouns and Antecedents

Directions Read each sentence. Write another sentence with a pronoun that refers to the underlined noun(s).

1. <u>Africa</u> is a lush and fertile continent.

   _____

2. <u>Jane Goodall</u> visited <u>chimps</u> in a zoo.

   _____

3. <u>Buku</u> is a large male gorilla.

   _____

4. <u>J.J. and I</u> are going to the circus.

   _____

5. <u>Helen and Andrew</u> fed the chimp with a <u>baby's bottle</u>.

   _____

6. I wrote a <u>story</u> about Jane Goodall.

   _____

7. <u>Phil and I</u> joined an organization to help protect the chimps.

   _____

8. <u>Mr. Blackwell</u> is a scientist who studies <u>monkeys</u>.

   _____

Home Activity Your child learned how to correctly use pronouns and antecedents in writing. Have your child write a letter to a relative using pronouns and antecedents correctly.

Name _____

The Chimpanzees I Love
TEST PREPARATION

Pronouns and Antecedents

Directions Mark the letter of the pronoun that agrees with the antecedent to complete each sentence.

1. My friends wanted to see the chimps at the zoo, so I bought _____ tickets.
   A you
   B him
   C her
   D them

2. Kiki is a female chimp, and _____ weighs eighty-three pounds.
   A her
   B she
   C we
   D it

3. Gorillas and bonobos are African apes, and _____ are disappearing very fast.
   A they
   B he
   C it
   D you

4. You should never tease an animal, even when _____ are just playing.
   A it
   B you
   C us
   D them

5. We knew that the animal shelter was nearby, but we had trouble finding _____.
   A you
   B her
   C them
   D it

6. My brother and I ran from Fanni as she chased _____.
   A he
   B us
   C I
   D she

7. Some people used to dress chimps and teach _____ tricks.
   A her
   B them
   C us
   D it

8. My sister loves stuffed animals, so I bought _____ one as a gift.
   A they
   B it
   C he
   D her

9. I told Mom that chimps can learn sign language, but she did not believe _____.
   A me
   B she
   C they
   D we

10. Washoe's son wanted to play with Rory and me, but _____ did not trust him.
    A her
    B them
    C we
    D him

Home Activity Your child prepared for taking tests on pronouns and antecedents. Write a person's name, a noun, and a compound noun such as *Mom and Sam* on paper. Have your child write one sentence using the correct pronoun to refer to each antecedent you wrote.

Name _____

The Chimpanzees I Love
CUMULATIVE REVIEW

Pronouns and Antecedents

Directions Circle the pronoun in each sentence and underline its antecedent.

1. Mrs. Taylor teaches about chimps because they are an endangered species.
2. Kent and James want to visit Africa so they can see chimps in a natural habitat.
3. The forest ranger just started working at the park, but he knows about the plants and animals.
4. Mike is driving to the wildlife shelter, and Carrie is following him.
5. Mrs. Taylor brought photos of Kenya and showed them during the presentation.
6. Scientists have tried to teach sign language to chimps, but Kaatu could not learn it.
7. One chimp tried to use a computer, but she failed.
8. Charlotte and Terry were hiding, but Tiki found them.
9. Emily was hoping Pete would go with her to the lecture.
10. Jesse and Owen's parents sat with them at the lecture.

Directions Write the pronoun that agrees with the antecedent. Underline the antecedent to which the pronoun refers.

> me   she   he   we   they

11. Jane Goodall gave a lecture; then _____ answered questions.
12. As Jon listened attentively, _____ took notes.
13. Laurel and Mike arrived later, so _____ sat in the back of the hall.
14. I wanted Dr. Goodall to call on _____.
15. _____ students were responsible for refreshments.

Home Activity Your child reviewed pronouns and antecedents. Have your child find correct pronoun and antecedent usage in an ad or a catalog.

68 Unit 4 Week 2 **Day 5**   **Grammar and Writing Practice Book**

Name _____

Black Frontiers

DEVELOP THE CONCEPT

Possessive Pronouns

Pronouns that show ownership are called **possessive pronouns.** A possessive pronoun and its antecedent must agree in number and gender. Before you use a possessive pronoun, ask yourself whether the antecedent is singular or plural. If the antecedent is singular, decide whether it is masculine, feminine, or neuter. Then choose a pronoun that agrees.

Possessive Pronouns
My/mine, your/yours, his, her/hers, its, our/ours, their/theirs

- *My, your, her, our,* and *their* are always used with nouns.
  I did my report on the Exodusters.
- *Mine, yours, hers, ours,* and *theirs* stand alone.
  Which science project is yours?
- *His* and *its* can be used with nouns or can stand alone.
  His report discussed life on the frontier.
  The report on frontier life was his.
- Do not use an apostrophe with a possessive pronoun.

Directions Underline the possessive pronoun in each sentence.

1. My history book tells the story of the Buffalo Soldiers.
2. Some black settlers moved to Nebraska and started their new lives.
3. Our country has a rich cultural heritage.
4. Does your family come from Louisiana?
5. Former slaves knew that as sharecroppers, freedom would never be theirs.
6. As an American, the right to life, liberty, and the pursuit of happiness is mine.
7. The pioneer woman gathered buffalo chips for her cooking fire.

Directions Circle the pronoun in ( ) that completes each sentence.

8. John Lewis Solomon knew (their, his) rights.
9. The dog stayed in (our, its) warm bed on the floor.
10. For early black homesteaders, loneliness was part of (their, theirs) lives.
11. The woman worked to build (hers, her) home with mud walls.

Home Activity Your child learned about possessive pronouns. Make up or read a sentence with a possessive pronoun. Ask your child to identify the possessive pronoun.

Grammar and Writing Practice Book   Unit 4 Week 3 **Day 2** **69**

Name _____

Black Frontiers

APPLY TO WRITING

Possessive Pronouns

> his   her   its   your   their

Directions Rewrite each sentence, replacing the underlined noun or noun phrase with a possessive pronoun from the box.

1. After the Civil War, former slaves stayed in the South hoping <u>the former slaves'</u> circumstances would change.

   _____
   _____

2. A sharecropper found that the <u>sharecropper's</u> debts were never paid off.

   _____
   _____

3. A farm woman made soap and shampoo out of plants for <u>the woman's</u> family.

   _____
   _____

4. A goat warmed a <u>goat's</u> hooves on the roof of the house.

   _____
   _____

Directions Write sentences about African American history. Include a possessive pronoun in each sentence. Underline the possessive pronoun.

_____
_____
_____
_____
_____
_____

Home Activity Your child learned how to use possessive pronouns in writing. Ask your child to write several sentences about what it would have been like to live in the United States shortly after the Civil War. Ask your child to use at least three possessive pronouns and to point them out.

70 Unit 4 Week 3 **Day 3**   **Grammar and Writing Practice Book**

Name _____

Black Frontiers
TEST PREPARATION

Possessive Pronouns

Directions Circle the letter of the possessive pronoun in the sentence.

1. He studied the tactics of the Tenth Cavalry in his history book.
   A he
   B tenth
   C book
   D his

2. Black soldiers had been farmers, blacksmiths, cooks, and carpenters in their towns before they enlisted in the cavalry.
   A black
   B they
   C their
   D towns

3. Each black community celebrated Emancipation Day as its own special holiday.
   A each
   B its
   C own
   D day

4. Our class admires the former slaves who started new lives after the Civil War.
   A them
   B Our
   C former
   D who

5. A pioneer woman brewed tea from wild grasses on her farm.
   A a
   B pioneer
   C she
   D her

6. His great-grandparents were among the pioneers who persevered under harsh conditions.
   A His
   B who
   C pioneers
   D harsh

7. You can learn about the strength of African Americans' spirit as you study their history.
   A You
   B African Americans'
   C the
   D their

8. Following the Civil War, every American could exclaim, "Freedom is mine."
   A every
   B American
   C the
   D mine

9. John Solomon could pay for his own transportation on the boat.
   A his
   B the
   C John Solomon
   D boat

10. Nicodemus and Dunlap were two of the communities of African Americans in our country.
    A our
    B two
    C of
    D Nicodemus and Dunlap

Home Activity Your child prepared for taking tests on possessive pronouns. With your child, read a short article in the newspaper. Have your child circle any possessive pronouns he or she finds in the article.

Grammar and Writing Practice Book Unit 4 Week 3 **Day 4** **71**

Name _____

Black Frontiers

CUMULATIVE REVIEW

Possessive Pronouns

Directions Underline the possessive pronoun in each sentence.

1. Our class is studying the plight of slaves after the Civil War.
2. Slaves read about Israelites who were delivered out of their bondage.
3. Nicodemus marked its legacy by becoming a National Historic Landmark.
4. Can you remember the date of Emancipation Day from your study of history?
5. Exodusters were named for their exodus, or departure, from the South.
6. The Army paid every black man in the cavalry thirteen dollars a month for his service.
7. Anne claimed that the idea to make soap from the yucca plant was hers.
8. We should respect our civil rights and be willing to fight for them.
9. Mr. Singleton hoped two hundred families would settle on his Cherokee reservation.
10. That book about African Americans is mine.

Directions Replace the underlined word or words with a possessive pronoun. Write the possessive pronoun.

11. African American athletes owe a great deal of <u>African American athletes'</u> success to athletes such as Satchel Paige. _____

12. A pioneer woman worked hard making a home for <u>a pioneer woman's</u> family. _____

13. The Exodusters left <u>the Exodusters'</u> homes in the South. _____

14. The small animal made <u>the small animal's</u> bed inside the home in cold weather. _____

15. Christine was happy that the story her teacher read aloud was <u>Christine's</u>. _____

Home Activity Your child reviewed possessive pronouns. Ask your child to look at a story in a magazine or newspaper and provide the correct possessive pronouns for at least three proper nouns.

72 Unit 4 Week 3 **Day 5**

Grammar and Writing Practice Book

Indefinite and Reflexive Pronouns

Indefinite pronouns may not refer to specific words. They do not always have definite antecedents: Someone needs to press her uniform.
Some common indefinite pronouns are listed below:

Singular Indefinite Pronouns
someone, somebody, anyone, anybody, everyone, everybody, something, no one, either, each

Plural Indefinite Pronouns
few, several, both, others, many, all, some

- Use singular verb forms with singular indefinite pronouns and plural verb forms with plural indefinite pronouns: Everyone wants to fly a spaceship. Few do it well.

Reflexive pronouns reflect the action of the verb back upon the subject. Reflexive pronouns end in -self or -selves: The cadet wanted to see the planet himself.

Singular Reflexive Pronouns
himself, herself, myself itself, yourself

Plural Reflexive Pronouns
ourselves, yourselves, themselves

- There are no such words as hisself, theirself, theirselves, or ourself.

Directions Underline the correct indefinite pronoun in ( ) to complete each sentence.

1. Does (few, anyone) see the horizon?

2. (Several, Everyone) believe that the planet is habitable.

3. (Many, No one) have volunteered to travel to the M-class planet.

4. If (others, somebody) pilots the spaceship, Tom will go along.

Directions Write the correct reflexive pronoun to complete each sentence.

> yourselves   myself   himself   ourselves

5. We may have to defend _____ against the alien life forms.

6. I _____ will represent Earth Command.

7. You cannot allow _____ to be captured by the aliens.

8. Tom blamed _____ for putting the crew in danger.

Home Activity Your child learned about indefinite and reflexive pronouns. Ask your child to circle three indefinite pronouns in a newspaper article and identify whether each is singular or plural.

Name _____

Space Cadets
APPLY TO WRITING

Indefinite and Reflexive Pronouns

Directions Write a sentence using the indefinite pronoun and the correct verb in ( ).

1. everyone (listen, listens)
_____
_____

2. several (learns, learn)
_____
_____

3. no one (understands, understand)
_____
_____
_____

4. both (walk, walks)
_____
_____
_____

5. somebody (is, are)
_____
_____

6. everything (fall, falls)
_____
_____
_____

Directions Write a sentence using the reflexive pronoun.

7. myself
_____
_____
_____

8. themselves
_____
_____
_____

Home Activity Your child learned how to use indefinite and reflexive pronouns in writing. Have your child write a note to his or her teacher using two indefinite or two reflexive pronouns and tell you which is which.

74 Unit 4 Week 4 **Day 3** Grammar and Writing Practice Book

Indefinite and Reflexive Pronouns

Directions Mark the letter of the pronoun(s) that complete each sentence.

1. Roger tried to fly the spaceship ____.
   A hisself
   B himself
   C yourself
   D ourselves

2. ____ is falling apart on our spaceship.
   A Others
   B Myself
   C Everything
   D Many

3. ____ have failed the training program.
   A Many
   B Somebody
   C No one
   D Yourself

4. The officers regard ____ as professional pilots.
   A anything
   B yourselves
   C herself
   D themselves

5. Claire taught ____ how to pilot a space cruiser.
   A yourself
   B herself
   C hisself
   D herselves

6. ____ enlist in the space cadet program to see the universe.
   A Ourselves
   B Both
   C Everyone
   D Somebody

7. The crew is lost because ____ knows how to set the coordinates.
   A nobody
   B many
   C themselves
   D both

8. If ____ volunteers for the spacewalk, ____ will be rewarded.
   A everyone, they
   B anyone, he or she
   C anyone, they
   D ourselves, we

9. ____ may have to prepare ____ for combat.
   A Many, they
   B Ourselves, he
   C Several, himself
   D You, yourselves

10. ____ want to do it ____ without the captain's help.
    A We, themselves
    B He, himself
    C We, ourselves
    D We, yourself

Home Activity Your child prepared for taking tests on indefinite and reflexive pronouns. Ask your child to use the reflexive pronouns *myself, yourself* and *himself* in sentences and explain to whom they refer back the action of the verb.

Indefinite and Reflexive Pronouns

Directions Underline the correct word in ( ) to complete each sentence.

1. Everyone (thinks, think) the captain is strange because he talks to himself.
2. Many of the space pilots (practices, practice) on the flight simulator.
3. Everybody (studies, study) the Space Cadet Training Guide.
4. The captain assures us that nothing (are, is) going to stop our journey.
5. Both of the boys (stumbles, stumble) onto the bridge.
6. (Several, One) of them have gone back to Earth for training.
7. The alarm is sounding because (many, something) is wrong!
8. (Both, Anyone) of the officers train to become Star Generals.
9. The aliens approach the landing party, but (few, nobody) panics.
10. (Everyone, Both) shows (their, his) best manners.

Directions Write the correct reflexive pronoun from the box to complete each sentence.

> yourself   myself   herself   themselves   ourselves

11. The First Officers designed the training program _____.
12. I am not interested in space travel _____.
13. We introduced _____ to Og and Mog.
14. Do not leave _____ open to an attack by the hostile aliens.
15. Molly prepares the officers' lunch _____.

Home Activity Your child reviewed indefinite and reflexive pronouns. Have your child make up a slogan for a favorite product using one indefinite pronoun or one reflexive pronoun.

Using Who and Whom

> The pronoun *who* is used as a subject.
>
>   Who planted the garden? (*Who* is the subject of the sentence.)
>   My sister is the only one who likes roses. (*Who* is the subject of the clause *who likes roses*.)
>
> The pronoun *whom* is used as the object of a preposition, such as *to, for,* and *from*, and as a direct object. Most often, *whom* will be a direct object in questions.
>
>   To whom did you send the flowers? (*Whom* is the object of the preposition *to*.)
>   This is a man whom I admire. (*Whom* is the direct object of the verb *admire* in the clause *whom I admire*.)
>   Whom did you invite? (*Whom* is a direct object.)
>
> You can check if *whom* should be used as a direct object. Change the word order so that the subject comes first. (*Whom* did you invite? You did invite *whom*?)

Directions Circle the pronoun in ( ) that correctly completes each sentence.

1. These are the inventors (who, whom) you should acknowledge.
2. Mr. Edison, (who, whom) was a fond father, nicknamed his children Dot and Dash.
3. Edison was the inventor (who, whom) wealthy investors supported.
4. The lab assistants were the ones (who, whom) built Edison's prototypes.
5. Edison worked with the assistants (who, whom) were best suited for the positions.
6. He is one of the people (who, whom) history honors as a brilliant inventor and scientist.
7. Give the data to the woman (who, whom) calls for it.
8. People (who, whom) own CD players can thank Edison for his inventions.

Directions Write *who* or *whom* to complete each sentence correctly.

9. Batchelor and Kruesi were two assistants to _____ Edison entrusted his work.
10. Edison believed negative results were valuable to a scientist _____ wanted to learn.
11. _____ stole Edison's heart and married him?
12. To _____ shall we award the patent for this clever invention?

Home Activity Your child learned about using *who* and *whom*. Have your child look through a magazine, point out the pronouns *who* and *whom*, and explain why each pronoun is used.

Name _____

Inventing the Future
APPLY TO WRITING

Using *Who* and *Whom*

Directions Choose *who* or *whom* to correctly complete each sentence. Then write this sentence and answer or explain it with another sentence or two.

1. A person who/whom I admire is _____.

2. To who/whom do I go for advice?

3. A person who/whom works hard is _____.

4. Who/Whom is a person from history I'd like to meet?

Directions Write two sentences about inventions you use every day. Use *who* or *whom* in each sentence.

5. _____

6. _____

Home Activity Your child learned how to use *who* and *whom* in writing. Ask your child to tell about the device in your home that he or she thinks is the most important invention. Ask your child to use *who* and *whom* at least once.

78 Unit 4 Week 5 **Day 3** **Grammar and Writing Practice Book**

Using Who and Whom

Directions Mark the letter of the pronoun that correctly completes the sentence.

1. Edison sold patents to those ___ wanted exclusive manufacturing rights.
   A whom
   B which
   C what
   D who

2. In 1876, Edison moved with his wife, ___ he married in 1871, to New York City.
   A whom
   B who
   C that
   D which

3. The investors knew ___ they would blame for the failure of the business.
   A him
   B them
   C whom
   D who

4. ___ thought up the idea for the telephone?
   A Whose
   B Which
   C Who
   D Whom

5. Alexander Graham Bell is the inventor ___ I admire the most.
   A whom
   B who
   C whose
   D which

6. ___ should I thank for inventing the electric light bulb?
   A Who
   B Whom
   C Whose
   D Why

7. Edison sold the electric pen to mapmakers ___ saw value in the device.
   A whose
   B what
   C whom
   D who

8. To ___ did Edison sell his Newark-based business?
   A whom
   B who
   C them
   D that

9. Edison was a man ___ loved catnaps.
   A whom
   B which
   C who
   D what

10. To ___ do we give credit for the invention of the incandescent bulb?
    A who
    B what
    C that
    D whom

Home Activity Your child prepared for taking tests on using *who* and *whom*. Have your child write a paragraph about inventions. Ask him or her to use the pronouns *who* and *whom* at least once.

Name _____

Inventing the Future
CUMULATIVE REVIEW

Using Who and Whom

Directions Circle the pronoun in ( ) that correctly completes each sentence.

1. Edison bragged about his "mockers" (who, whom) turned out inventions.
2. To (who, whom) did Edison give blueprints?
3. (Who, Whom) was known as the "Wizard of Menlo Park"?
4. Batchelor was the assistant (who, whom) posed in a photo taken with electric light.
5. (Who, Whom) did *Scientific American* interview about the phonograph?

Directions Write *who* or *whom* to complete each sentence correctly.

6. The inventor _____ improved the telephone also invented the phonograph.
7. Edison thought of _____ he could trust.
8. The scientist to _____ Bill was assigned was a brilliant statistician.
9. _____ is responsible for inventing the television?
10. _____ was present when the telephone transmitted Edison's faint voice?
11. The neighbor _____ lives down the street is an inventor.
12. Edison spoke to Batchelor, with _____ he had worked for many years.
13. I work with scientists, for _____ I have great respect.
14. Edison met a 16-year-old girl named Mary Stilwell _____ worked as a clerk.
15. At 23, Edison was a promising scientist _____ had a reputation as an electrical inventor.

Home Activity Your child reviewed using *who* and *whom*. Ask your child to say a sentence using *who* and another sentence using *whom* and to tell why these words are correctly used.

80 Unit 4 Week 5 **Day 5**   **Grammar and Writing Practice Book**

Name _____

The View from Saturday

DEVELOP THE CONCEPT

Contractions and Negatives

A **contraction** is a shortened form of two words. An **apostrophe** is used to show one or more letters have been left out. Some contractions are made by combining pronouns and verbs: I + will = I'll. Other contractions are formed by joining a verb and *not* or *have*: do + not = don't; should + have = should've.

- *Won't* and *can't* are formed in special ways (*can* + *not* = *can't*; *will* + *not* = *won't*).

Negatives are words that mean "no" or "not": *no, not, never, none, nothing.* Contractions with *n't* are negatives too. To make a negative statement, use only one negative word.

  No   He doesn't have no money.
  Yes   He doesn't have any money. *or* He has no money.

- Use positive words instead of negative ones in a sentence with *not.*

Negative	Positive	Negative	Positive
nobody	anybody, somebody	nothing	anything, something
no one	anyone, someone	nowhere	anywhere, somewhere
none	any, all, some	never	ever, always

Directions Write the letter of the two words used to form each contraction.

_____ 1. couldn't   A I am

_____ 2. would've   B would have

_____ 3. they're   C could not

_____ 4. I'm   D they are

Directions Write the contraction for each pair of words.

5. she + will = _____

6. did + not = _____

7. it + is = _____

8. will + not = _____

Directions Circle the word in ( ) that correctly completes each sentence.

9. No one has (never, ever) seen such a beautiful bride.

10. We couldn't find (nowhere, anywhere) to put all the gifts.

Home Activity Your child learned about contractions and negatives. Have your child find three contractions and three negatives in the newspaper comics and tell what words are used to form each contraction.

Grammar and Writing Practice Book   Unit 5 Week 1 Day 2 **81**

Name _____

The View from Saturday

APPLY TO WRITING

Contractions and Negatives

Directions Rewrite each sentence to make it a negative sentence. Change the underlined word to a contraction or a negative word.

1. Somebody gave the bride and groom a lovely present.
   _____

2. Are you going to get a new dress for the wedding?
   _____
   _____

3. I was told to attend the reception.
   _____

4. Aunt Peg said I will throw rice at the bride and groom.
   _____
   _____

5. The best man had somewhere to go.
   _____

6. The baker can make a five-layer cake.
   _____

Directions Have you ever attended a wedding? Write three sentences about your experience or write about how you imagine a wedding. Use contractions in two sentences. Make at least one sentence negative.

_____
_____
_____
_____
_____

Home Activity Your child learned how to use contractions and negatives in writing. Have your child write sentences about a relative, using contractions and negatives whenever possible.

82 Unit 5 Week 1 **Day 3**   **Grammar and Writing Practice Book**

Contractions and Negatives

Directions Mark the letter of the sentence that is written correctly.

1. A There wasn't no one left at the reception.
   B There was'nt nobody left at the reception.
   C There wasn't anyone left at the reception.
   D There wasnt anybody left at the reception.

2. A I dont never want to take dance lessons.
   B I don't ever want to take dance lessons.
   C I doesn't want to take dance lessons.
   D I don't want to take no dance lessons.

3. A None of my pens has ink.
   B None of my pens has no ink.
   C My pens hasn't no ink.
   D None of my pens hasn't ink.

4. A The photographer shouldn't take no more photos.
   B The photographer shouldn't never take more photos.
   C The photographer should never take no more photos.
   D The photographer shouldn't take more photos.

5. A They're not going to cut no cake yet.
   B They're not going to cut the cake yet.
   C Theyre not going to cut the cake yet.
   D They're never going to cut no cake yet.

6. A We've never seen nobody as pretty as the bride.
   B We've not seen no one as pretty as the bride.
   C We haven't seen anyone as pretty as the bride.
   D We haven't seen no one as pretty as the bride.

7. A Haven't you been to Florida?
   B Haven't you not been to Florida?
   C Haven't you never been to Florida?
   D Have'nt you ever been to Florida?

8. A You shouldn't never dance with Uncle Ernie!
   B You should not dance with Uncle Ernie never!
   C You shouldn't ever dance with Uncle Ernie!
   D You should'nt dance with Uncle Ernie!

Home Activity Your child prepared for taking tests on contractions and negatives. Read aloud three simple sentences from a magazine article one at a time. Ask your child to make each sentence negative.

Name _____

The View from Saturday
CUMULATIVE REVIEW

Contractions and Negatives

Directions Write the contractions for the underlined words in the sentences.

1. <u>They will</u> come over after the wedding. _____
2. You may have had enough cake, but I <u>have not</u>. _____
3. <u>I would</u> really like the cake to be chocolate. _____
4. <u>You have</u> been busy making plans for the wedding. _____
5. The groom says he <u>is not</u> nervous. _____
6. I <u>did not</u> want to be the ring bearer. _____
7. <u>She is</u> wearing the wedding dress her mother wore. _____
8. <u>We are</u> flying to Florida in the morning. _____
9. I <u>do not</u> want to leave my grandparents' house. _____
10. They <u>will not</u> put a centerpiece on the table. _____

Directions Circle the word in ( ) that correctly completes each sentence.

11. They won't (never, ever) forget this day.
12. We didn't see (no, any) presents.
13. She won't go (anywhere, nowhere) until the party is over.
14. Didn't (anybody, nobody) catch the bouquet?
15. He wouldn't let (no one, anyone) near the cake.
16. Nobody knows (anything, nothing) about the broken chair.
17. We can't go (nowhere, anywhere) after the party.
18. Dad couldn't eat (any, none) of the food.
19. He never said (nothing, anything) about the music.
20. I don't (never, ever) dance at weddings.

Home Activity Your child reviewed contractions and negatives. Have your child read aloud a page from a familiar story and change contractions into the words they are made of as he or she reads.

84 Unit 5 Week 1 **Day 5**   **Grammar and Writing Practice Book**

Name _____

Harvesting Hope

DEVELOP THE CONCEPT

Adjectives and Articles

An **adjective** is a word that describes a noun or pronoun. It tells what kind, how many, or which one.

We stood in the <u>crisp</u> air. The girls were <u>eager</u>. (what kind)
<u>Several</u> people came. <u>Four</u> women worked. (how many)
What was <u>that</u> noise? <u>These</u> ideas are good. (which ones)

The words *a*, *an*, and *the* are special adjectives called **articles**. They appear before nouns and other adjectives. Use *a* before a word that begins with a consonant sound. Use *an* before a word that begins with a vowel sound. Use *the* before words beginning with any letter.

<u>The</u> boy grew up in <u>a</u> home in Arizona. <u>An</u> old friend called me.

A **proper adjective** is formed from a proper noun. Proper adjectives are always capitalized.

They raised the <u>Mexican</u> flag.

Directions Underline the adjectives in the sentences once. Underline the articles twice.

1. Those eager supporters talked to leaders of the march.
2. A peaceful march was the goal.
3. Workers were welcomed into an inviting shelter.
4. A black eagle adorned the flag.
5. Tired workers hunched over the grapevines.
6. An irate landowner worried about that vineyard.
7. A ripe grape must be picked or it will rot.
8. Many people gathered at the ranch for friendly barbecues.

Directions Write *a*, *an*, or *the* to complete each sentence.

9. We planted _____ interesting garden last year.
10. Maria picked _____ artichoke from the garden.
11. He knew he was _____ most stubborn boy in class.
12. César Chávez did not believe he was _____ strong fighter.
13. To help _____ migrant workers, people boycotted certain crops.
14. Did you know that _____ raisin comes from a grape?

Home Activity Your child learned about adjectives and articles. Have your child underline three sentences in the newspaper and then circle the articles and other adjectives in the sentences.

Grammar and Writing Practice Book Unit 5 Week 2 **Day 2** **85**

Name _____

Harvesting Hope

APPLY TO WRITING

Adjectives and Articles

Directions Add a vivid adjective to describe each underlined noun.

1. In the summer, we enjoy _____ watermelon and _____ lemonade.

2. His uncle spun _____ stories for the children.

3. César's grandfather built an _____ house in Arizona.

4. On his first day at school, he sat in the _____ seat near his sister.

5. In California, the Chávez family lived in a _____ shed.

6. They could not work in the _____ weather.

7. _____ air seeped into the house, and the boys couldn't sleep.

8. In the first grade, César acted like a _____ boy.

9. The boy wore an old, _____ coat.

10. He had the _____ movements of an athlete.

Directions Rewrite the following sentences. Use a vivid adjective to describe each underlined noun.

11. The plant grew near the house.
_____
_____

12. The sun ripened the grapes.
_____
_____

13. The men yelled at the marchers.
_____
_____

14. Heroes serve as models for us.
_____
_____

Home Activity Your child learned how to use adjectives and articles in writing. Have your child write a paragraph about something he or she did at school. Have your child review the paragraph and add three adjectives to describe nouns.

86 Unit 5 Week 2 **Day 3**   **Grammar and Writing Practice Book**

Adjectives and Articles

Directions Mark the letter of the adjective in each sentence.

1. The migrant workers spent hours in the fields.
   A migrant
   B workers
   C fields
   D spent

2. On the march, Chávez developed painful blisters on his feet.
   A march
   B painful
   C blisters
   D feet

3. Police officers locked strong arms to keep marchers from crossing.
   A keep
   B from
   C arms
   D strong

4. His blisters bled and ruined his sturdy shoes.
   A blisters
   B ruined
   C bled
   D sturdy

5. Joyous marchers rallied under the cry *Sí Se Puede*.
   A rallied
   B Joyous
   C under
   D *Sí Se Puede*

6. Those grapes spoiled during the strike.
   A spoiled
   B strike
   C Those
   D grapes

7. The landowners foolishly resisted the persistent Chávez.
   A persistent
   B foolishly
   C resisted
   D landowners

8. The workers sought their basic rights.
   A workers
   B sought
   C basic
   D rights

9. Every night of the march became a rally.
   A night
   B Every
   C became
   D rally

10. People stopped eating California grapes.
    A People
    B stopped
    C grapes
    D California

Home Activity Your child prepared for taking tests on adjectives and articles. Ask your child to explain what articles and adjectives are and to point out examples of each in something he or she has written.

Name _____

Harvesting Hope
CUMULATIVE REVIEW

Adjectives and Articles

Directions Underline the adjectives in the sentences once. Underline the articles twice.

1. Religious leaders offered help to the protestors.
2. As an American citizen, I have certain rights.
3. It was an honor to hear the eloquent speakers.
4. That stunning victory surprised everyone.
5. A crowd celebrated under starry skies.

Directions Write *a, an,* or *the* to complete each sentence.

6. César suffered from _____ aching leg and _____ fever after the march.

7. _____ final contract offered higher wages and better conditions.

8. Chávez drove to Beverly Hills to meet with _____ landowners.

9. People sang _____ victory song at the celebration.

Directions Add a vivid adjective to describe each underlined noun.

10. _____ <u>supporters</u> celebrated César's thirty-eighth birthday.

11. Ten thousand _____ <u>people</u> arrived in Sacramento.

12. Chávez fought for the first signed contract for farmworkers in _____ <u>history</u>.

13. Speakers addressed the _____ <u>crowd</u> in Spanish.

14. _____ <u>determination</u> paid off for Chávez and his followers.

15. Farmworkers trusted <u>Chávez</u> because he was _____.

Home Activity Your child reviewed adjectives and articles. Have your child find three sentences with adjectives in a magazine article. Ask him or her to replace the adjectives with different adjectives.

88 Unit 5 Week 2 **Day 5**   **Grammar and Writing Practice Book**

Name _____

River to the Sky

DEVELOP THE CONCEPT

Demonstrative Adjectives

The adjectives *this, that, these* and *those* are called **demonstrative adjectives**. They describe which one or which ones. *This* and *that* modify singular nouns. *These* and *those* modify plural nouns. *This* and *these* refer to things that are close by. *That* and *those* refer to things farther away.

This river is teeming with fish, but that one over the hill is not.
These animals look like those animals we saw by the road yesterday.

Do not use *here* or *there* after *this, that, these,* or *those*.

No: This here river runs fast. That there river is slow and quiet.
Yes: This river runs fast. That river is slow and quiet.

Do not use *them* in place of *these* or *those*.

No: Them animals are hiding in the trees.
Yes: Those animals are hiding in the trees.

Directions Underline the words in ( ) that complete the sentences correctly.

1. Tall grasses and willowy trees grow beside (these, this) flowing river.

2. (That, These) bushes and hedges guard the foothills of the great mountain.

3. A family of gazelles rests in (that, that there) patch of towering elephant grass.

4. The clouds remembered (this, those) peaceful times when they were a part of Earth.

5. (These, That) dense jungles are filled with huge trees and creeping vines.

6. The sun will take (this here, this) river up to the sky.

7. Will you go with me to (that, these) village near the foot of the great mountain?

8. (These, That) chimpanzees followed (those, that) gorillas into the jungle.

9. (This, These) river and (them, these) animals are part of a great African myth.

10. (Those, This) leopard is not as fast as (those, that) cheetahs.

Home Activity Your child learned about demonstrative adjectives. Ask your child to name the four demonstrative adjectives and use each one in a sentence.

Grammar and Writing Practice Book   Unit 5 Week 3 **Day 2** **89**

Name _____

Demonstrative Adjectives

Directions Replace the underlined word(s) with the correct demonstrative adjective. Use the clue in ( ). Rewrite each sentence.

1. (far away) The path will lead to <u>the</u> great river near the horizon.

   _____

   _____

2. (nearby) <u>The</u> map will show us how to reach the small lakes.

   _____

   _____

3. (nearby) We must be lost because <u>the</u> trees do not look familiar.

   _____

   _____

4. (far away) If <u>one</u> herd begins to migrate, <u>the other</u> herds will migrate too.

   _____

   _____

5. (nearby) <u>The</u> myth explains how <u>the</u> rivers were formed.

   _____

   _____

Directions The continent of Africa is full of plant and animal life. Write three sentences about Africa. Use at least one demonstrative adjective in each sentence.

_____

_____

_____

Home Activity Your child learned how to use demonstrative adjectives in writing. Together look for demonstrative adjectives in ads. Have your child explain why each demonstrative adjective was used.

Name _____

River to the Sky

TEST PREPARATION

Demonstrative Adjectives

Directions Mark the letter of the correct answer that completes each sentence.

1. The exodus of animals began with ____ pride of lions beyond the tall grasses.
   A this
   B that
   C them
   D that there

2. In the night sky, ____ stars look like winking eyes.
   A them
   B those
   C this
   D those there

3. I walked quickly through ____ bushes on the other side of the lake.
   A this
   B that
   C these
   D those

4. ____ myth that I am reading gives a voice to the sun, the sky, and the animals.
   A This
   B That
   C This here
   D Those

5. The animals drink daily from ____ flowing waters.
   A these here
   B that
   C this
   D these

6. ____ rare trees and flowers will not survive without the River.
   A Those
   B This
   C Them
   D That

7. There are great lessons to be learned from ____ myth.
   A those
   B this here
   C this
   D these

8. Before I read ____ story, I had never read a myth from Africa.
   A this here
   B these
   C that
   D them

9. ____ sandy dunes were once grassy fields.
   A These
   B Them
   C That
   D Those here

10. ____ grass bundles were cut from ____ fields beyond the stream.
    A This, those
    B Those, those
    C These, them
    D That, those

Home Activity Your child prepared for taking tests on demonstrative adjectives. Give your child singular and plural nouns and have him or her name the two demonstrative adjectives that can be correctly used with each noun.

Grammar and Writing Practice Book   Unit 5 Week 3 **Day 4** **91**

Name _____

River to the Sky

CUMULATIVE REVIEW

Demonstrative Adjectives

Directions Underline the words in ( ) that complete the sentences correctly.

1. The River yearned to leave (that, this) earth and travel to the skies.
2. Do you want to pick some of (those, them) flowers in the meadow?
3. (Those, This) land is rich and fertile, but (those, that) land is dry.
4. You should wear (this, these) sunglasses to protect your eyes.
5. (That, Those) leopards are beautiful but dangerous.
6. Did you see (that there, that) cheetah running through the grasses?
7. Take (this, these) photo of the Sahara to show your teacher.
8. All of (these, this) African rivers have interesting names.
9. (This, Those) particles of water formed fluffy white clouds.
10. (These, That) large gorilla is the strongest of the family.
11. I enjoyed reading (this, this here) myth about the River and the Sky.
12. I swam in some of (that, these) small lakes.

Directions Write the sentences correctly.

13. This here book explains the formation of the Sahara.

    _____
    _____

14. Mrs. Palmer read us stories about them African cultures.

    _____
    _____

15. That there herd of antelope has traveled far to reach water.

    _____
    _____

Home Activity Your child reviewed demonstrative adjectives. Have your child find sentences with demonstrative adjectives in a favorite book and tell whether each sentence tells about something nearby or far away.

Name **Sebastian Mazzini**

100

DEVELOP THE CONCEPT

Comparative and Superlative Adjectives

Comparative adjectives compare two people, places, things, or groups. Add -er to most short adjectives to make their comparative forms. Use *more* with longer adjectives. **Superlative adjectives** compare three or more people, places, things, or groups. Add -est to most short adjectives to make their superlative forms. Use *most* with longer adjectives.

Adjective	Comparative	Superlative
bright	bright**er**	bright**est**
expensive	**more** expensive	**most** expensive

Never use *more* or *most* with -er and -est.
  No: more longer, most amazingest
  Yes: longer, most amazing

When adding -er or -est to an adjective that ends in e, drop the e: *large, larger, largest*. If the adjective ends in y, change the y to i: *happy, happier, happiest*. If the adjective ends in a single consonant, double the consonant: *hot, hotter, hottest*.

Some adjectives have irregular comparative and superlative forms: *good, better, best; bad, worse, worst; much, more, most; little, less, least*.

Directions Write the comparative and superlative forms of each adjective.

Adjective   Comparative   Superlative
fine   1. finer   2. finest
easy   3. easier   4. easiest
plentiful   5. more plentiful   6. most plentiful
sad   7. sadder   8. saddest
little   9. lesser   10. leastest
positive   11. more positive   12. most positive
brilliant   13. more brilliant   14. most brilliant

Directions Circle the correct form of the adjective to complete each sentence.

15. My sister's ring is (shinier, more shinier) than mine.

16. The diamond looked (spectacularer, more spectacular) than the sapphire.

17. John was the (most careful, carefullest) prospector of all the miners.

18. Can she make this gold leaf (more thin, thinner) than it is now?

Home Activity Your child learned about using comparative and superlative adjectives. Have your child scan a magazine article, select five adjectives, and tell the comparative and superlative forms of each adjective.

Grammar and Writing Practice Book   Unit 5 Week 4 **Day 2** 93

Name: Sebastian Mazzini

Gold
APPLY TO WRITING

Comparative and Superlative Adjectives

Directions Write a sentence about the given topic. Use your own words and the adjective form in ( ).

Example: the shiny earrings (superlative)
Sue had the shiniest earrings of all because she polished them.

1. beautiful necklace (superlative)
   My mom had the most beautiful necklace of all.

2. disappointed girl (comparative)
   My sister was more disappointed than her friend who had too much homework.

3. valuable jewelry (superlative)
   My mom's collection of jewelry includes the most valuable jewelry of all.

4. heavy box (comparative)
   Those boxes are heavier than the other ones.

5. important artist (superlative)
   I'm the most important artist of all of the artists that ever lived.

6. bright color (comparative)
   That color is brighter than darker colors.

7. precious possession (superlative)
   Lou had the most precious possession of all.

8. high price (comparative)
   That price is higher than the cost of 2 soup cans combined.

Home Activity Your child learned how to use comparative and superlative adjectives in writing. Have your child write a paragraph comparing two musical groups. Ask your child to use at least one comparative and one superlative adjective.

Name _____

DEVELOP THE CONCEPT

Adverbs

> An **adverb** tells *how, when,* or *where* something happens. An adverb may appear before or after the verb it modifies, or between the parts of a verb phrase.
>
> He sleepily watched the stars. (how)
> She will soon go on a journey. (when)
> The luggage was piled everywhere. (where)
>
> Adverbs such as *too, very, quite, really, so, nearly,* and *almost* can modify adjectives and other adverbs.
>
> I was too early. We left very quickly.
>
> **Comparative adverbs** compare two actions. Add *-er* to many adverbs to make them comparative. **Superlative adverbs** compare three or more actions. Add *-est* to many adverbs to make them superlative. If an adverb ends in *-ly,* use *more* or *most* instead of *-er* or *-est.*
>
> loud   louder   loudest
> carefully   more carefully   most carefully
>
> Some adverbs do not follow the rules for comparative and superlative forms: *well, better, best; badly, worse, worst; much, more, most.*

Directions Underline the adverb or adverbs in each sentence.

1. The canopy of stars twinkled very brightly in the sky.
2. The students stepped outside and discussed Socrates.
3. We must make plans now.
4. The marketplace is almost empty.
5. Ishaq missed his home badly.
6. We can eat first and study later.
7. Eventually, the new library will be built here.
8. He walked slowly down the street.

Directions Circle the word in ( ) that completes the sentence correctly.

9. Hunayn did not (more high, highly) value the gold he was paid.
10. The scholar searched (more seriously, more serious) for wisdom than he had before.
11. She thought that Aristotle wrote (well, best) of all the writers.
12. Merchants (more proudly, proudly) wore their traditional robes.

Home Activity Your child learned about adverbs. Give your child three verbs, such as *run, play,* and *swim,* and have your child make up a sentence using each verb and adding an adverb to modify the verb.

Grammar and Writing Practice Book   Unit 5 Week 5 **Day 2** **97**

Name _____

The House of Wisdom

APPLY TO WRITING

Adverbs

Directions Rewrite each sentence. Add an adverb that answers the question in ( ).

1. The student will leave the House of Wisdom. (When?)

2. He read ancient Greek, one word at a time. (How?)

3. Ishaq sat and listened to the scholars. (Where?)

4. I read about Hippocrates and other Greek thinkers. (When?)

5. My mother searched for me in the marketplace. (How?)

6. The ship arrived after a long journey. (Where?)

7. He learned about other cultures on the expedition. (How?)

8. Ishaq wanted to be a learned man like his father. (When?)

Home Activity Your child learned how to use adverbs in writing. Have your child write three sentences about his or her favorite activity, using an adverb in each sentence.

98 Unit 5 Week 5 **Day 3**   **Grammar and Writing Practice Book**

Name _____

The House of Wisdom
TEST PREPARATION

Adverbs

Directions Mark the letter of the word or phrase that best completes each sentence.

1. We listened ____ to the scholars discussing Plato.
   A more close
   B closely
   C most closer
   D close

2. He spoke Arabic ____ than she did.
   A well
   B best
   C good
   D better

3. This ship sails ____ than that one.
   A faster
   B most faster
   C fastest
   D more faster

4. She was ____ anxious to leave.
   A real
   B really
   C realer
   D more real

5. We expected them at noon, but they arrived ____.
   A soonest
   B soon
   C sooner
   D more soon

6. Ishaq's father embraced him ____.
   A warmer
   B more warmly
   C warm
   D warmly

7. He ____ studied the birds and the stars.
   A patiently
   B more patient
   C most patiently
   D patient

8. He noticed that the stars gleamed ____ when he was at sea.
   A very brighter
   B very brightly
   C more bright
   D more brighter

9. He ____ watched the elephants gather at the Ganges River.
   A more curious
   B most curiously
   C curiously
   D curious

10. I do not know how to ride a camel ____.
    A good
    B very good
    C goodly
    D very well

Home Activity Your child prepared for taking tests on adverbs. Ask your child to find three adverbs in an ad or catalog and write the comparative and superlative forms for each adverb.

Grammar and Writing Practice Book   Unit 5 Week 5 **Day 4** **99**

Name _____

The House of Wisdom
CUMULATIVE REVIEW

Adverbs

Directions Underline the adverb or adverbs in each sentence.

1. Now he recklessly raced his horse and wildly threw his javelin.
2. Ishaq traveled quite cautiously through the sandstorms of the Sahara.
3. Finally, they arrived wearily in Cordova.
4. Everywhere he went, he paid handsomely for books.
5. There he bought the trinkets that the children happily offered.
6. We barely slept while on the rickety boat.
7. The merchant yelled more loudly than the screeching monkeys.
8. He read the manuscripts more thoroughly than the letters.
9. It's a good thing I can ride camels so well.
10. Tonight we gratefully eat the food we purchased at the marketplace.
11. Later we will sing together outside.
12. We are quite happy here.
13. We will sleep very well.

Directions Use the adverbs from the box to complete the paragraph.

| better | tomorrow | swiftly | there | eventually |

(14) _____ morning we go on a new and strange journey! (15) Our ship will _____ sail to Egypt. (16) _____ we will meet a seller of rare books. (17) He treats his books _____ than the seller in India does. (18) _____ we will return with a treasure!

Home Activity Your child reviewed adverbs. Ask your child to say three sentences using the verb *skate* and the correct forms of the adverb *badly* (*badly, worse, worst*).

100 Unit 5 Week 5 Day 5   Grammar and Writing Practice Book

Name _____

Don Quixote
DEVELOP THE CONCEPT

Modifiers

Adjectives, adverbs, and prepositional phrases are **modifiers**, words or groups of words that tell more about, or modify, other words in a sentence. Adjectives modify nouns and pronouns. Adverbs modify verbs, adjectives, or other adverbs. Prepositional phrases can act as adjectives or adverbs.

As Adjective The windmills <u>on the hill</u> were huge.
As Adverb The horse galloped <u>up the hill</u>.

- To avoid confusion, place modifiers close to the words they modify. Adjective phrases usually come right after the word they modify. Adverb phrases may appear right after a verb or at the beginning of a sentence.
- The meaning of a sentence can be unclear if the modifier is misplaced.
  No: We read about a knight who battled giants <u>in class</u>.
  Yes: We read <u>in class</u> about a knight who battled giants.
- The position of *only* in a sentence can affect the sentence's entire meaning. Place *only* directly before the word or words it modifies.
  Example: <u>Only</u> he saw giants. (Nobody else saw them.)
  He <u>only</u> saw giants. (He didn't do anything except see.)
  He saw <u>only</u> giants. (He saw nothing else.)

Directions Write *adverb, adjective,* or *prepositional phrase* to identify each underlined modifier. Write *adjective* or *adverb* to identify how a prepositional phrase is used.

1. The squire rode <u>behind the knight</u>. _____

2. Don Quixote wore pieces of <u>rusty</u> armor. _____

3. <u>Bravely</u> he battled the windmills. _____

4. The lady <u>in his dream</u> was named Dulcinea. _____

Directions Each sentence has a misplaced modifier. Rewrite the sentence and put the word or phrase where it belongs.

5. I sat and thought about knights in the kitchen.

_____

6. Don Quixote only wanted Dulcinea, no one else.

_____

Home Activity Your child learned about modifiers. With your child, read a favorite story. Ask your child to point out several adjectives, adverbs, and prepositional phrases and explain what those words or phrases are modifying.

Grammar and Writing Practice Book Unit 6 Week 1 **Day 2** **101**

Name _____

Don Quixote

APPLY TO WRITING

Modifiers

Directions Add adjectives, adverbs, and prepositional phrases to these sentences. Use the modifiers to create a more specific, interesting picture.

1. A horse ran.
   _____

2. The sun rose.
   _____

3. Sancho saddled the donkey.
   _____
   _____

4. The knight rode.
   _____

Directions Write a sentence using each prepositional phrase below. Make sure the connection between the phrase and the word or words it modifies is clear.

5. on his head
   _____

6. in the town
   _____
   _____

7. across the fields
   _____
   _____

8. with sad eyes
   _____
   _____

Home Activity Your child learned how to use modifiers in writing. Have your child look at something he or she has written and point out modifiers. Have your child decide if any modifiers could be replaced or added to improve the writing.

102 Unit 6 Week 1 **Day 3**   **Grammar and Writing Practice Book**

Modifiers

Directions Mark the letter of the item that correctly identifies the underlined word or words in each sentence.

1. The birds awakened at dawn.
   A adjective
   B adverb
   C prepositional phrase/adjective
   D prepositional phrase/adverb

2. Don Quixote fought the giants bravely.
   A adjective
   B adverb
   C prepositional phrase/adjective
   D prepositional phrase/adverb

3. Sancho Panza was his faithful squire.
   A adjective
   B adverb
   C prepositional phrase/adjective
   D prepositional phrase/adverb

4. A knight in full armor needs his squire's help.
   A adjective
   B adverb
   C prepositional phrase/adjective
   D prepositional phrase/adverb

5. Sancho held tightly to Don Quixote's ankle.
   A adjective
   B adverb
   C prepositional phrase/adjective
   D prepositional phrase/adverb

6. They left the inn in the early afternoon.
   A adjective
   B adverb
   C prepositional phrase/adjective
   D prepositional phrase/adverb

Directions Mark the letter of the sentence that has a misplaced modifier.

7. A Don Quixote wanted to be a knight who battled dragons.
   B The peasants laughed when they saw the old man on his horse.
   C Several angry merchants did not laugh at his challenge.
   D We learned about peasants who revolted on the Internet.

8. A We put the books on those shelves by the door.
   B The stories tell about kings, knights, and ladies.
   C I loved the book about giants in our library.
   D Only John has read the whole series.

Home Activity Your child prepared for taking tests on modifiers. Copy a paragraph from a newspaper article, leaving blanks where modifiers go. Ask your child to suggest possible modifiers for the blanks. Compare with the original paragraph.

Name _____

Don Quixote
CUMULATIVE REVIEW

Modifiers

Directions Underline the prepositional phrase in each sentence. Write *adverb* or *adjective* to identify how the prepositional phrase is used.

1. We played in the park in the afternoon. _____
2. The sun on my head is hot and uncomfortable. _____
3. Jorge rides his horse along the trail. _____
4. Watch that man by the tree. _____
5. You can see clearly in the bright light. _____
6. The woman with the white scarf smiled warmly. _____

Directions Underline the adjectives, adverbs, and prepositional phrases in each sentence. The number in ( ) tells how many modifiers a sentence contains. (Do not underline the articles *a*, *an*, and *the*.)

7. The two knights shared a meager dinner under the trees. (3)
8. Sancho slowly poured cold water into the pot. (3)
9. He made a thick stew that had very little meat in it. (4)
10. ngry peasants quickly stuffed the bread in their mouths. (3)
11. An a of giants was marching west through the valley. (3)

Directions Identiy the misplaced modifier in each sentence. Rewrite the sentence, and put the modifier where it belongs. Underline the modifier.

12. Joyce only ate the bread—no other food.

_____

13. We could see cattle grazing in the distance with binoculars.

_____

_____

14. The man waved to me with a beard.

_____

Home Activity Your child reviewed modifiers. Have your child use a magazine article to show you adjectives, adverbs, and prepositional phrases that make the writing specific and interesting.

104 Unit 6 Week 1 **Day 5**   **Grammar and Writing Practice Book**

Name _____

Ancient Greece

DEVELOP THE CONCEPT

Conjunctions

> A **conjunction** is a word that is used to join words, phrases, or sentences.
> **Coordinating conjunctions** such as *and, but,* and *or* are used to combine two or more subjects, predicates, or sentences to make compound subjects, predicates, or sentences.
>   Maggie <u>and</u> Deb are marathon runners.
>   Katie will run five miles <u>or</u> swim 50 laps tomorrow.
>   Gerry wanted to see the Greek play, <u>but</u> he was ill.
>
> **Subordinating conjunctions** such as *because, if, then, when, although, before,* and *after* are used to link dependent clauses and independent clauses in complex sentences.
>   He gets good grades <u>because</u> he studies. <u>When</u> she speaks, everyone listens.

Directions Underline the correct conjunction in ( ).

1. Wrestling (but, and) boxing were part of the ancient Olympic games.

2. He could throw a javelin, (or, but) he could not throw a discus.

3. Were the games held in Athens (or, but) Olympia?

4. I wanted to attend the Olympic trials, (and, but) I could not get a ticket.

5. The ancient Greeks developed both a democratic system of government (or, and) a system of trial by jury.

6. Listen carefully to the words of this song, (and, or) you will learn about legendary Greek heroes.

7. Is the play a comedy (and, or) a tragedy?

8. Samantha read "The Tortoise and the Hare," (but, or) she did not like it.

Directions Underline the conjunction in each sentence. Write *CC* if it is a coordinating conjunction and *SC* if it is a subordinating conjunction.

9. If you read Aristotle's works, you will learn his ideas about happiness.   _____

10. Children offered toys to Apollo and Artemis.   _____

11. Although Greece was a land of democracy, people still owned slaves.   _____

12. Greek men often held meetings, but the women did not attend.   _____

Home Activity Your child learned about conjunctions. Have your child find three conjunctions in a favorite book, tell whether they are coordinating or subordinating conjunctions, and explain how he or she knows.

Grammar and Writing Practice Book   Unit 6 Week 2 **Day 2** **105**

Name _____

Ancient Greece

APPLY TO WRITING

Conjunctions

Directions Rewrite the following paragraph. Combine related subjects, predicates, or sentences using conjunctions to make the paragraph smoother. Where appropriate, drop repeated words or replace repeated nouns with pronouns. Make sure subjects and verbs agree.

(1) Our class learned about the science of ancient Greeks. Our class learned about the philosophy of ancient Greeks. (2) The teacher asked me to write about a famous Greek scientist. The teacher asked Bobby to write about a famous Greek scientist. (3) I wondered if I should choose Hippocrates. I wondered if I should choose Archimedes. (4) I chose Archimedes. Bobby chose Hippocrates. (5) Archimedes was able to lift a ship from the water. This happened because he applied what he learned about levers. (6) Hippocrates studied medicine. Hippocrates developed the Hippocratic oath. (7) Doctors today take the Hippocratic oath. They take this oath when they enter the profession. (8) The discoveries of Archimedes have influenced our lives today. The discoveries of Hippocrates have influenced our lives today.

_____
_____
_____
_____
_____
_____
_____
_____
_____
_____
_____
_____
_____
_____
_____
_____

Home Activity Your child learned how to use conjunctions in writing. Have your child write four sentences about the Olympics, using either a coordinating or subordinating conjunction in each sentence and identifying each as one or the other.

106 Unit 6 Week 2 **Day 3**   **Grammar and Writing Practice Book**

Name _____

Ancient Greece
TEST PREPARATION

Conjunctions

Directions Mark the letter of the conjunction(s) that best complete each sentence.

1. We learned about Zeus and Hermes ____ we studied Greek mythology.
   A but
   B when
   C or
   D although

2. Ancient Greek paintings were beautiful ____ colorful.
   A after
   B before
   C and
   D but

3. ____ Athens and Sparta had been enemies, they joined forces to fight Persia.
   A Then
   B But
   C When
   D Although

4. Some ancient statues look unrealistic, ____ many Greek statues look natural.
   A but
   B or
   C if
   D because

5. ____ Anaxagoras presented his hypotheses, the world believed the moon made its own light.
   A Then
   B Before
   C If
   D But

6. ____ my father arrives, we can order Greek ____ Chinese food.
   A Because, and
   B But, or
   C If, but
   D When, or

7. Aesop's fables are enjoyed by adults ____ children alike.
   A but
   B and
   C because
   D then

8. ____ we finish our homework early, we can watch a Greek play.
   A If
   B Then
   C Although
   D But

9. I understood American politics ____ government better ____ I studied Aristotle.
   A or, although
   B but, after
   C and, but
   D and, after

10. Public gyms were common in ancient Greece ____ Greeks valued exercise ____ health.
    A after, or
    B because, and
    C or, and
    D although, but

Home Activity Your child prepared for taking tests on conjunctions. Ask your child to look through a newspaper article and find three coordinating conjunctions and three subordinating conjunctions.

Grammar and Writing Practice Book   Unit 6 Week 2 **Day 4**   **107**

Name _____

Ancient Greece
CUMULATIVE REVIEW

Conjunctions

Directions Underline the correct conjunction in ( ).

1. The modern Olympic games are held every two years, (and, before) they alternate between summer and winter.

2. My cousin was scheduled to run the marathon, (because, but) he sprained his ankle a day before the race.

3. (Before, And) you study American government, read Aristotle's thoughts about liberty.

4. Did the modern Olympics begin in 1896 (or, and) 1897?

5. Jill chose to read about Hippocrates (or, because) she wants to be a doctor.

6. Chariot races must have been exciting (but, after) dangerous.

7. (If, After) the Dark Ages ended, Athens (and, but) Sparta became powerful city-states.

8. (If, Before) Pericles came to power, only wealthy people served in government.

9. (If, When) Rome defeated the last Greek kingdom, the Hellenistic age was over.

10. We study ancient Greece today (because, but) Greek culture influenced the world.

Directions Underline the conjunction in each sentence. Write *CC* if it is a coordinating conjunction and *SC* if it is a subordinating conjunction.

11. The Greeks developed drama and literature. _____

12. I read some of Aesop's fables when I returned home. _____

13. The teacher wanted ten students for the Greek drama, but only six students volunteered. _____

14. Will you come to the Ancient Greece exhibit, or will you stay at home? _____

15. The Roman Empire grew after the Romans conquered the Greeks. _____

16. Although a fable teaches a lesson, it can still be entertaining. _____

17. She could run for miles, but she could not swim a single lap. _____

18. If you like Greek myths, you will like the one explaining why spiders weave webs. _____

Home Activity Your child reviewed conjunctions. Together listen to 30 seconds of a news broadcast and have your child write some conjunctions he or she hears during that time.

108 Unit 6 Week 2 **Day 5** **Grammar and Writing Practice Book**

Commas

> You already know that **commas** are used in compound sentences, after the greeting and closing in a letter, and in series of three or more words, phrases, or sentences. Here are other uses of commas.
>
> - After an introductory word or phrase, such as *well, yes,* or *by the way*
>   Well, I suppose that suggestion makes the most sense.
> - To set off a noun of direct address
>   Mrs. Gleason, may I take your coat? I warned you, Meg, to stay home.
> - After a dependent clause at the beginning of a sentence
>   When they come to visit, they always bring a tasty treat.
> - Before and/or after an appositive—a noun or noun phrase describing another noun
>   The main course, spicy chicken, was delicious.
> - Before and after interrupting words or phrases
>   The buffet, as they promised, was loaded with food.
> - Between a day of the week and a month and between a date and a year
>   Today is Tuesday, March 14. Their wedding was on January 17, 2006.
> - Between the street address and the city and between the city and the state in an address. Do not use a comma before the ZIP code.
>   My school is at 1432 Cross Street, Chicago, IL.

Directions Read the following parts of a letter. Add commas where they are needed.

1. How is your family Mr. Gleason?

2. My parents look forward to your visit as you know.

3. Sunday April 5 2007

4. Dear Mr. Gleason

Directions Add commas where they are needed in the sentences.

5. The Lakeview an expensive restaurant requires reservations.

6. We like hamburgers milkshakes and chow mein.

7. After we saw the movie we went out to dinner.

8. Our neighbors moved to 53 West Birman Street Birmingham New York.

Home Activity Your child learned about commas. Have your child look at a page of a favorite book, point out the commas, and explain why each comma is used.

Commas

Directions Rewrite the sentences, adding commas where necessary.

1. Mrs. Lin an eager guest took a covered dish to the party.

2. Mrs. Gleason would you like to sit next to the window?

3. Yes I like Chinese food but I like Mexican food better.

4. When they visited the Midwest the family dined in Lakeview Illinois.

5. Our mail was forwarded from our address at 101 North Street Madison Wisconsin.

6. Meg piled rice shrimp chicken and vegetables onto her plate.

Directions Write one sentence with an appositive and one sentence with an interrupting word or phrase. Be sure to use commas correctly.

7. (appositive) _____

8. (interrupting word or phrase) _____

Home Activity Your child learned how to use commas in writing. Have a short conversation with your child. Ask your child to write the conversation and put commas where they are needed.

Name _____

The All-American Slurp
TEST PREPARATION

Commas

Directions Mark the letter of the sentence in which commas are used correctly.

1. A The Lins bought furniture, a dart board, and a jigsaw puzzle, for their house.
   B The Lins bought furniture, a dart board, and a jigsaw puzzle for their house.
   C The Lins bought furniture, a dart board and, a jigsaw puzzle for their house.
   D The Lins bought furniture a dart board and a jigsaw puzzle for their house.

2. A Mrs. Beacon, did you invite the Lins to your party on Saturday?
   B Mrs. Beacon did you invite, the Lins to your party, on Saturday?
   C Mrs. Beacon, did you, invite the Lins to your party on Saturday?
   D Mrs. Beacon, did you invite the Lins, to your party on Saturday?

3. A Chow mein, as you may know is not really Chinese food.
   B Chow mein as you, may know, is not really Chinese food.
   C Chow mein as you may know, is not really Chinese food.
   D Chow mein, as you may know, is not really Chinese food.

4. A Her brother, an athlete, made the junior high baseball team.
   B Her brother an athlete made the junior high baseball team.
   C Her brother an athlete, made the junior high baseball team.
   D Her brother an, athlete made the junior high baseball team.

5. A Mr. Lin practiced English, and became fluent.
   B Mr. Lin practiced English, and he became fluent.
   C Mr. Lin practiced English and, became fluent.
   D Mr. Lin practiced English, and, became fluent.

6. A Her mother took her to buy her first pair of jeans, on March, 4 2006.
   B Her mother took her to buy her first pair of jeans on, March 4, 2006.
   C Her mother took her to buy her first pair of jeans on March 4, 2006.
   D Her mother took her to buy her first pair of jeans, on March 4 2006.

7. A Mr. Lin an engineer was quite systematic about everything he did.
   B Mr. Lin, an engineer was quite systematic about everything he did.
   C Mr. Lin an engineer, was quite systematic about everything he did.
   D Mr. Lin, an engineer, was quite systematic about everything he did.

8. A We set the table with, rice bowls, chopsticks and soy sauce, at dinner.
   B We set the table with, rice bowls, chopsticks, and soy sauce, at dinner.
   C We set the table with rice bowls, chopsticks and soy sauce, at dinner.
   D We set the table with rice bowls, chopsticks, and soy sauce at dinner.

Home Activity Your child prepared for taking tests on commas. Ask your child to write a paragraph about trying a new food for the first time. Have your child use commas in at least three different ways.

Grammar and Writing Practice Book

Commas

Directions Read the following parts of a letter. Add commas where they are needed.

1. Dear Mrs. Lin
2. Superior CO 80027
3. Monday February 19
4. Thank you for the birthday gift Mrs. Lin.

Directions Add commas where they are needed in the sentences.

5. Because we didn't have any flour Mother did not make potstickers.
6. Excuse me may we have a table for four?
7. Dad got a promotion a higher salary and increased confidence.
8. Well let's draw straws to see who will set the table for dinner.

Directions Rewrite the sentences, adding commas where necessary.

9. When the waiter brought the soup we weren't sure how to eat it.

10. I tried to read the menu but it was in French.

11. Father a systematic man tries to be prepared for all situations.

12. The waiter brought water lemon slices and extra napkins to the table.

Home Activity Your child reviewed commas. Choose a piece of junk mail. Ask your child to find at least three commas in it and identify how they are used.

Quotations and Quotation Marks

> A **direct quotation** gives a speaker's exact words. Begin each quotation with a capital letter and enclose it in **quotation marks**. Use commas to set off words that introduce, interrupt, or follow a direct quotation. Place the end punctuation or the comma that ends the quotation inside the quotation marks.
> "I am preparing food for the festival," she said. "What kind of food?" I asked.
>
> Do not begin the second part of an interrupted quotation with a capital letter. Set off the interrupting phrase with commas.
> "Remember," said Mother, "don't be late."
>
> If the interrupted quotation is two complete sentences, use a period and a capital letter.
> "Please make tortillas," I begged. "They taste great!"
>
> An **indirect quotation** is a quotation that is reworded instead of being quoted directly. It does not need quotation marks.
> Father said he would sing at the festival.

Directions Write *I* if the sentence is punctuated or capitalized incorrectly. Write *C* if the sentence is correct.

1. Do you live in a royal palace?" the boy asked. _____
2. "No, she replied. "I live in a whitewashed cottage." _____
3. The street vendor yelled, "Buy a tortilla pancake!" _____
4. "The pochtecas" Grandfather said, "Are merchants who may also be spies." _____
5. "Spies!" I exclaimed. "Is it dangerous?" _____

Directions Add quotation marks to each sentence as needed.

6. Take these cocoa beans to the market, Mother advised. Don't stop along the way!

7. What an adventure! declared the boy.

8. Look out your window at night, Mother said. You may see a pochteca leaving the city.

9. Are they richer than the nobles? I asked.

10. Tonight we celebrate my birthday, Sheri said. Are you coming to my party?

Home Activity Your child learned about quotations and quotation marks. Have your child explain the difference between a direct quotation and an indirect quotation.

Name _____

The Aztec News
APPLY TO WRITING

Quotations and Quotation Marks

Directions Add quotation marks, punctuation, and capitalization. Indicate the change of a speaker with a paragraph indent. Add a quotation of your own at the end.

(1) If you were born to a noble family during the time of the Aztecs explained Ms. Dennis you might be sent to a calmecac school. (2) There you would learn to become a judge or a general she said. (3) Unfortunately she added you would not be allowed to live at home. (4) Where did the commoners' children attend school asked Jenny. (5) They attended a telpochcalli school answered Ms. Dennis. (6) Although they were expected to sleep at the school she continued they were free to eat meals with their families. (7) Which type of school would you rather attend she asked. (8) _____

Home Activity Your child learned how to use quotations and quotation marks in writing. Have your child listen to a conversation and write a quotation from that conversation, using quotation marks, punctuation, and capitalization correctly.

Name _____

The Aztec News
TEST PREPARATION

Quotations and Quotation Marks

Directions Mark the letter of the answer that correctly completes each sentence.

1. "The noblemen wore feather ____ said Mr. Wills.
   A capes,
   B capes."
   C capes,"
   D capes",

2. "If a commoner is caught committing a crime," warned the judge, ____ will be severely punished."
   A he
   B He
   C "He
   D "he

3. The historian stated, "Tenochtitlán was a beautiful city, completely surrounded by ____
   A water."
   B water.
   C water"
   D water

4. ____ and streets crisscrossed the city," he said.
   A canals
   B "canals
   C "Canals
   D Canals

5. ____ yelled the Eagle warrior.
   A "Watch out!"
   B "Watch out"
   C "Watch out
   D "Watch out"!

6. "Do you want to walk or travel by ____ she asked.
   A canoe"
   B canoe?
   C canoe"?
   D canoe?"

7. ____ the nobleman said, "our lives are not always easy."
   A "You see"
   B "You see,"
   C "You see
   D "you see,"

8. "Our great temple has two shrines," the priest ____ "They honor our gods of sun and rain."
   A said,
   B said!
   C said.
   D said

9. "Unfortunately," sighed the woman, ____ nobles are allowed in the Great Square."
   A "Only
   B "only
   C Only
   D only

10. "If you want to buy a trinket, go to the market," the porter said. ____ is just up ahead."
    A "It
    B It
    C it
    D "it

Home Activity Your child prepared for taking tests on quotations and quotation marks. Ask your child to find two quotations in a newspaper and rewrite them as indirect quotations.

Grammar and Writing Practice Book   Unit 6 Week 4 **Day 4** 115

Quotations and Quotation Marks

Directions Add quotation marks and punctuation to each sentence as needed.

1. At the party I said we will serve hot chocolate

2. Our teacher said the Aztecs knew how to throw a party

3. Your jade earrings are lovely June said

4. The musician said that he would play a traditional song after the feast

5. Can you paddle a canoe she asked

6. Did you read this article about Aztec culture asked Mrs. Bennett It's very interesting

7. Beth said she had read it yesterday

8. Grandmother whispered Lake Texcoco shimmers like a large emerald

Directions Rewrite each sentence, adding quotation marks, capitalization, and punctuation as needed.

9. The Aztec warriors used stones, spears, and arrows said Mr. Evans.

10. When the Spaniards fell into the lake I explained they could not swim because of their heavy armor.

11. Look at this armband the curator said you can see Aztec markings.

12. The child asked how we made the beads.

Home Activity Your child reviewed quotations and quotation marks. Ask your child three questions and have him or her write a response to each in the form of a quotation.

Name _____

Punctuation

DEVELOP THE CONCEPT

Where Opportunity Awaits

> You have already learned about punctuation such as commas, quotation marks, and end marks. Here are some other kinds of punctuation:
>
> - A **semicolon** (;) can be used to separate the two parts of a compound sentence when they are not joined by a comma and a conjunction.
>   Southerners migrated to the North; they often took the train.
> - Semicolons separate items in a series if commas are already used in the series.
>   The soccer team included Adam Hoyt, sophomore; Matthew Thomas, senior; and Joshua John, junior.
> - A **colon** (:) is used after the salutation in a business letter and to separate the hours and minutes in expressions of time.
>   Dear Mrs. Smith: 10:30 P.M.
> - Colons introduce a list and set off a speaker's name in a play.
>   I did the following chores: wax the car, clean my room, and sweep the porch.
>   SANDI: Hello there!
> - A **dash** (—) sets off information that interrupts the flow of a sentence.
>   Southerners—they included my relatives—suffered in the winter weather.
> - A **hyphen** (-) is used in certain compound words, such as compound adjectives before nouns; spelled-out numbers; and some two-word nouns.
>   a well-dressed man   fifty-four students   self-esteem
> - **Parentheses** ( ) set off additional information that is not essential.
>   The documentary will air on television next month. (Check your local listings.)
> - Parentheses enclose numbers or letters within a sentence.
>   She made a list of things to buy: (A) toothbrush, (B) clothes, (C) books.

Directions Add semicolons, colons, dashes, hyphens, or parentheses where they belong.

1. We visited the following states Georgia, Alabama, and Tennessee.

2. The play begins at 800 P.M. See Theater Notes for more information.

3. Our neighbors were Mr. Jones, a printer Mr. Smith, a blacksmith and Mr. Heath, a butcher.

4. The Thomases lived in a crowded apartment they shared it with another family.

5. Being a free man how he loved the sound of that was a boost to his self esteem.

6. EMILY Then where did they go?

    JOHN They went to Chicago.

Home Activity Your child learned about punctuation. Have your child scan a page of a book and identify at least three different punctuation marks. Ask your child to explain the uses of the punctuation marks.

Grammar and Writing Practice Book   Unit 6 Week 5 **Day 2** **117**

Name _____

Where Opportunity Awaits

APPLY TO WRITING

Punctuation

Directions Match each number in the first column with the letter of the related words in the second column. Then write the new sentences, using a colon or a semicolon.

_____ 1. Migrants needed the following   A they also seemed terribly long.

_____ 2. Winters in the North were cold   B jobs, housing, and friends.

_____ 3. Dear Mr. Mayor   C tickets, water, and a book.

_____ 4. Bring these items on the train   D I am writing about the ghetto.

1. _____

2. _____

3. _____

4. _____

Directions Add hyphens, dashes, colons, and semicolons to the following sentences. Rewrite the sentences.

5. As an ex Southerner, I miss the warm weather in January however, I like the North.

_____

6. We departed at 300 for the train station the 345 train is always on time.

_____

7. John Carter his friends call him Chip comes from Mississippi.

_____

Home Activity Your child learned how to use punctuation in writing. Copy a paragraph in a story, leaving out the punctuation. Ask your child to read the paragraph and tell where to add punctuation and why.

Punctuation

Directions Mark the letter that identifies the correct punctuation for each sentence.

1. The next train to Pittsburgh leaves at 1012.
   A The next train;
   B Pittsburgh:
   C The next train—to Pittsburgh
   D 10:12.

2. Harry wrote a letter to his well known cousin.
   A well-known
   B Harry—
   C wrote a letter;
   D to his cousin:

3. Blacks from the South often made less money they paid more for rent.
   A from the South;
   B from the South:
   C made less money;
   D made less money—

4. *The Philadelphia Enquirer* listed available jobs, unfortunately, he couldn't read.
   A jobs;
   B The Philadelphia Enquirer
   C *Enquirer*—listed
   D jobs:

5. Kyle visited the following cities Nashville, Memphis, and Knoxville.
   A Kyle—
   B Nashville; Memphis;
   C cities:
   D visited;

6. The Great Migration our neighbor remembers it brought many people north.
   A Migration-
   B —our neighbor remembers it—
   C Migration:
   D many people:

7. A half million people moved to the North during the Great Migration.
   A people:
   B North;
   C half-million
   D North—

8. The Great Migration was stimulated by jobs. See chart on page 42.
   A See: chart on page 42.
   B See chart; on page 42.
   C (See chart on page—42.)
   D (See chart on page 42.)

9. More than twenty five people signed up for the history lecture.
   A people:
   B twenty-five
   C people;
   D signed up;

10. Dear Mr. Ruiz
    A Ruiz:
    B :Ruiz
    C Ruiz;
    D Ruiz—

Home Activity Your child prepared for taking tests on punctuation. Have your child write a paragraph about the Great Migration of the 1900s. Ask your child to use a dash, a hyphen, a colon, and a semicolon in the paragraph.

Grammar and Writing Practice Book Unit 6 Week 5 **Day 4** **119**

Name _____

Where Opportunity Awaits

CUMULATIVE REVIEW

Punctuation

Directions Add semicolons, colons, dashes, hyphens, or parentheses where they belong.

1. The Thomas family moved to Chicago they arrived on a train.

2. His brand new job required him to be at work at 600 in the morning.

3. Train routes determined where many migrants relocated routes were called "chains."

4. Dear Mr. Harrison I would like to schedule an appointment.

5. The Thomas children study the following English, history, and science.

6. The dock workers included the following Jim, a Chicagoan Bill, an Ohioan and Tim, a Southerner.

7. MARTHA What day will you be arriving?

   MARY Our train will arrive on Saturday.

8. It can take time to adjust to a new city in the end, it is worth it.

9. To whom it may concern The railroad company needs additional employees.

10. School starts promptly at 815 A.M.

11. Mr. Thomas's neighbors included David, an usher Karl, a deliveryman and Mike, a shipyard worker

12. Boysenberry ice cream they sell it only at Kraft's is wonderful.

13. Black Southerners they were determined to read went to night school.

14. Many Southerners had family in the North they decided to move north too.

15. Chicago was a well known destination for Southerners. See photographs on page 9.

Home Activity Your child reviewed punctuation. Have your child write a letter to a friend describing what it would be like to move to a new place. Ask your child to use two semicolons and two colons in the letter.

120 Unit 6 Week 5 **Day 5**   **Grammar and Writing Practice Book**

Grammar Extra Practice

Name _____

Old Yeller
EXTRA PRACTICE

Four Kinds of Sentences

Directions Write *D* if the sentence is declarative. Write *IN* if the sentence is interrogative. Write *IM* if the sentence is imperative. Write *E* if the sentence is exclamatory.

1. Old Yeller was a stray dog. _____
2. I won't come any closer! _____
3. Don't forget the ax, Travis. _____
4. Arliss did not want to empty his pockets. _____
5. Will you leave that snake alone? _____
6. A bear is coming! _____
7. Take that lizard outside. _____
8. How much wood do you need, Mama? _____
9. Arliss was always getting into trouble. _____
10. Teach him how to kill snakes. _____

Directions Put a period, a question mark, or an exclamation mark at the end of each sentence to show what kind of sentence it is.

11. Will you keep an eye on your little brother _____
12. Arliss is holding the bear cub's leg _____
13. Old Yeller saved us all _____
14. Should we tell Papa about the bear _____
15. The snake is slithering toward you _____
16. When will you come home _____
17. It's time to feed the dog _____
18. I was so scared _____
19. Did you hear a noise _____
20. Let's eat dinner _____

Mother Fletcher's Gift

EXTRA PRACTICE

Subjects and Predicates

Directions Draw a line between the complete subject and the complete predicate in each sentence.

1. Mother Fletcher shopped at the market every Monday.
2. The officer's family dined with Mother Fletcher.
3. She wore a pretty green dress on Christmas Day.
4. Christmas lights twinkled from every window.
5. The brave officer has a wife and daughter.

Directions Underline the simple subject and circle the simple predicate.

6. The paramedic checked Mother Fletcher's pulse.
7. Officer O'Brien keeps the streets of Harlem safe.
8. Aunt Betsy baked ham and sweet potatoes for Christmas dinner.
9. A warm friendship had formed between the officer and the old woman.
10. Tinsel was hanging from every branch of her Christmas tree.

Directions Write *F* after fragments. Write *R* after run-ons. Write *S* after sentences.

11. Knitted a green sweater for Mike. _____
12. The children reread stories about Santa they know them by heart. _____
13. Streets of Harlem lively at night. _____
14. Colorful Christmas decorations adorn the houses in the neighborhood. _____
15. Everyone knew about Mother Fletcher she was a legend. _____
16. Officer O'Brien became a police officer because he wanted to help people. _____

Grammar and Writing Practice Book

Name: Sebastian Mazzini

Viva New Jersey
EXTRA PRACTICE

Independent and Dependent Clauses

Directions Write *IC* after each independent clause and *DC* after each dependent clause.

1. Because she was lonely. __DC__
2. Lucinda went to school every day. __IC__
3. The dog followed her. __IC__
4. When the sun went down. __DC__
5. After they left the house. __DC__

Directions Write *IC* if the group of underlined words is an independent clause and *DC* if it is a dependent clause.

6. __IC__ Fried bananas are served in Cuba where banana crops are grown.
7. __DC__ Although many Cubans attempt it, the journey to America is treacherous.
8. __DC__ Marlene is learning English when she can find the time.
9. __IC__ Since he came to America, Jorge has learned many new things.
10. __IC__ Maria could not learn English before the school year started.
11. __DC__ If you are learning a new language, you should practice speaking it every day.
12. __IC__ Papa walked to his job because Mama needed the car.
13. __DC__ The Vasquez family is happy in America although they miss their friends in Cuba.
14. __DC__ After Gloria started school, she made friends quickly.
15. __IC__ They lived in a small apartment because housing was scarce.

Directions Underline the independent clause and circle the dependent clause in each sentence.

16. When the immigrants moved to New Jersey, they could not find a home.
17. Although Lucinda missed her grandmother, she loved America.
18. Lucinda was on her way to school when she saw a dog tied to a post.
19. Since the dog looked abandoned, Lucinda took it home.
20. After she cleaned up the dog, it ran around the apartment.

Name _Sebastian Mazzini_

Saving the Rain Forests
EXTRA PRACTICE

Compound and Complex Sentences

Directions Identify each sentence as *simple, compound, complex,* or *compound-complex.*

1. Although the blooms are lovely, you may not pick them.
   complex   -1

2. The lush forest always feels cool in the morning and hot in the afternoon.
   simple

3. Take a jacket with you, or you may regret it after the sun goes down.
   compound

4. Some plants are useful, but others are poisonous.
   compound

5. Alexandra could not move very quickly because the brush was so thick.
   complex complex

6. They finally made it back to camp, and everyone had dinner.
   compound

7. Leigh Ann took out her camera and photographed the colorful birds.
   simple

Directions Join each pair of simple sentences to make a compound sentence. Use a comma and the conjunction *and, but,* or *or.* Write the compound sentence.

8. Jeremy loves hiking. He hikes almost every weekend.
   Jeremy loves hiking, and he hikes almost every weekend.

9. Jeremy usually hikes ten miles. Today he will hike only five miles.
   Jeremy usually hikes ten miles, but today he will hike only five miles.

10. Will he hike with a partner? Does he prefer going with a group?
    Will he hike with a partner or does he prefer going with a group.

Grammar and Writing Practice Book   Unit 1 Week 4 **125**

Name _Sebastian Mazzim_   3/24/15

When Crowbar Came
EXTRA PRACTICE

Common and Proper Nouns

Directions Write *P* if the underlined noun is a proper noun. Write *C* if it is a common noun.

1. My grandparents live in Albany. __P__
2. They visit us on the Fourth of July. __P__
3. A crow snatched the man's hat. __C__
4. We ate vegetables from the garden. __C__
5. Broccoli is my favorite vegetable. __C__

Directions Underline the proper nouns and circle the common nouns.

6. Tilly saw a black crow on her windowsill.
7. Mrs. Johnston told Luke that it would make a good pet.
8. Mother named the bird Licorice.
9. It ate the rotten apples that had fallen to the ground.
10. New York is home to many animals.
11. Crowbar became a good friend over the years.
12. Craig filled the feeder with seed.
13. Mr. Tyler writes stories on his computer.
14. The scenes outside the window are his inspiration.
15. Dr. Wang picked up the money and took it to the National Bank.

Directions Replace the common nouns in ( ) with proper nouns. Be sure to use appropriate capitalization.

16. (friend) __Adam__ has never been to (city) __New York__.
17. (title) __Mrs.__ Janet Gordon was born in (country) __America__.
18. (relative) __George__ lives in (state) __Tennessee__.

126 Unit 1 Week 5   Grammar and Writing Practice Book

Regular and Irregular Plural Nouns

Directions Write the plural form of the noun.

1. city _____
2. life _____
3. bush _____
4. sister-in-law _____
5. tomato _____

Directions Circle the correct plural form of the nouns in ( ).

6. For breakfast, we ate wild (berrys, berries) and biscuits.
7. The smoke from the campfire kept the (flys, flies) away.
8. Marty made up stories about aliens in other (galaxys, galaxies).
9. The (nightes, nights) were windy and cold.
10. We sat on the (roofs, rooves) of our cars to watch the eclipse.
11. Did I take enough (photoes, photos) of the meteor shower?
12. Mike made three (wishes, wishs) on the shooting stars.
13. His (feet, foots) were wet, and his shoes were ruined.
14. The (oxes, oxen) worked in the field next to our campsite.
15. We forgot our (radioes, radios), so we did not know the weather forecast.

Directions Write the plural form of the noun in parentheses.

16. We used _____ (match) for our lanterns.
17. The _____ (child) could see the stars clearly.
18. Emile showed us _____ (video) about Saturn.
19. With our _____ (knife), we whittled sticks for roasting marshmallows.
20. We focused our _____ (telescope) on the Big Dipper.

Name _____

Dinosaur Ghosts
EXTRA PRACTICE

Possessive Nouns

Directions Underline the correct possessive noun in ( ) to complete each sentence.

1. The (moon's, moons') rays let us see at night.

2. The (viewers', viewer's) moods lifted when they saw the falling star.

3. Last (years', year's) trip to New Mexico was in October.

4. By the end of the day, (Marcos', Marco's) nose was sunburned.

5. Two (rangers', ranger's) trucks were parked by the road.

Directions Write the possessive noun in each sentence. Write *S* if it is a singular possessive noun. Write *P* if it is a plural possessive noun.

6. The Junior Paleontologist Club received the good news from the school's Web site.
   _____

7. Some of the students' parents went on the trip as chaperones.
   _____

8. The students would work with Dr. Turner's team of scientists.
   _____

9. The drive to New Mexico's canyons was long but exciting.
   _____

10. The boys' gear was placed in one bunkhouse. _____

11. The girls' gear was placed in another. _____

12. The scientists' tools were unpacked, and the students began digging.
    _____

13. That paleontologist's predictions were correct. _____

14. The river's edge was littered with bones! _____

15. The students rarely asked for the researchers' help. _____

128 Unit 2 Week 2   **Grammar and Writing Practice Book**

Action and Linking Verbs

Directions Write *A* if the underlined word is an action verb. Write *L* if the underlined word is a linking verb. Write *PN* if the underlined word is a predicate nominative.

1. Julie <u>was</u> a gifted seamstress and baker. _____
2. Aaron <u>hammered</u> the red hot metal. _____
3. The children <u>play</u> hopscotch all afternoon. _____
4. Anna <u>became</u> competent with a needle and thread. _____
5. Nellie is the fastest <u>horse</u> in the stable. _____

Directions Underline each action verb. Circle each linking verb.

6. The handmade candles were warm and greasy.
7. Ben scratched at the dirt with a hoe.
8. Liz sketched the old barn with a piece of charcoal.
9. The air smells fresher in the country.
10. Josie and Walt paddled the canoe down the river.

Directions Circle *A* if the verb is an action verb. Circle *L* if it is a linking verb.

	A	L
11. Jake was an apprentice for a blacksmith.	A	L
12. Every day he walked to the smithy from his house.	A	L
13. The smithy appeared hot and dusty.	A	L
14. The blacksmith pounded on the anvil.	A	L
15. Jake pumped the bellows.	A	L
16. Smoke filled the room.	A	L
17. He wore heavy leather gloves.	A	L
18. It seemed the perfect job for Jake.	A	L

Subject-Verb Agreement

Directions Write *Yes* if the subject and the verb in the sentence agree. If they do not agree, write *No* and the correct form of the verb.

1. The trucks moves slowly along the road. _____
2. Uncle Ray removes the lens from the telescope. _____
3. Paul place a cool cloth on his forehead. _____
4. The spaceship flies to the moon every week. _____
5. His eyes is hidden behind the sunglasses. _____
6. She is writing about the moon. _____
7. Missions to the moon needs to be carefully planned. _____

Directions Underline the verb in ( ) that agrees with the subject.

8. (Is, Are) Kathy sketching the Earth or the moon?
9. The reporters (point, points) their cameras toward the governor.
10. The sun (stream, streams) across the landing pad.
11. Six passengers in the back (struggle, struggles) to stay awake.
12. Brian (save, saves) every penny for the lunar journey.
13. Both Kevin and Meg (study, studies) for the astronomy test.
14. Asteroids and meteors (races, race) across the galaxy.
15. Many people (prefers, prefer) to watch a sunrise rather than a sunset.
16. One girl (know, knows) where to find the North Star.
17. The class (walk, walks) together slowly through the planetarium.
18. The planets in our solar system (orbit, orbits) around the sun.
19. Astronauts (is, are) trained for space missions.
20. The entire tour group (listen, listens) attentively to the guide.

Name _____

Egypt

EXTRA PRACTICE

Past, Present, and Future Tenses

Directions Identify the tense of each underlined verb. Write *present*, *past*, or *future*.

1. We <u>will study</u> about Egypt next semester. _____
2. I <u>read</u> the book about mummies last week. _____
3. Ms. Randolph <u>works</u> at the Egyptology exhibit. _____
4. Our class <u>rode</u> the bus to the museum. _____
5. We <u>will view</u> an actual mummy! _____
6. Thomas <u>learned</u> about the pyramids. _____
7. I <u>will buy</u> a video about pharaohs. _____
8. Eva <u>looks</u> at the mummy through the glass. _____
9. Archaeologists <u>will find</u> more facts about Egypt. _____
10. We <u>walked</u> through the exhibit in two hours. _____

Directions Complete each sentence. Write the given verb in the tense indicated in ( ).

11. The scientists _____ for interesting artifacts in the pyramids. (search; future)
12. Mr. Blair _____ us about ancient Egypt. (teach; present)
13. The bricks _____ in the desert sun. (bake; past)
14. The camel _____ from the well outside the city. (drink; present)
15. Frank and Eric _____ their report on mummies. (present; future)
16. The Pharaoh's son _____ the next Pharaoh. (become; future)
17. The water from the well _____ sweet. (taste; past)
18. The sand _____ the nomad's tent. (cover; present)
19. The plants _____ if rain comes soon. (grow; future)
20. The Egyptian boy _____ dates, figs, and nuts. (eat; present)

Grammar and Writing Practice Book   Unit 2 Week 5 **131**

Principal Parts of Regular Verbs

Directions Write *present, present participle, past,* or *past participle* to identify the principal part used to form the underlined verb.

1. She has walked into the forest. _____
2. The jaguar snarls at the porcupine. _____
3. Carl had cooked his food before the storm. _____
4. The group traveled to the state park. _____
5. Stewart and I are waiting for the rain. _____
6. He chops branches with his hatchet. _____
7. Brian is listening for noises. _____
8. The plane crashed into the forest. _____

Directions Complete each sentence with the principal part used to form the given verb as indicated in ( ).

9. Charles _____ the ashes from the fire pit. (scoop/present tense)
10. She _____ her wilderness camp application yesterday. (mail/past tense)
11. He _____ his hatchet out of reach. (place/past participle with *has*)
12. The twig _____ as the man walks through the forest. (snap/present tense)
13. They _____ to the top of that hill. (climb/present participle with *are*)
14. We _____ all the matches in plastic. (wrap/past participle with *have*)
15. I got to my feet and _____ slowly back into the cave. (hobble/past tense)
16. The fire _____ the pile of dry twigs. (burn/present participle with *is*)
17. With great care, Brian _____ the match on a rock. (scrape/past tense)
18. He lifts a rock and _____ a melon open. (smash/present tense)
19. Claire and Beth _____ wood back to their camp. (carry/present participle with *are*)
20. Yesterday they _____ all the way around the lake. (hike/past participle with *had*)

Principal Parts of Irregular Verbs

Directions Write *present, present participle, past,* or *past participle* to identify the principal part used to form the underlined verb.

1. Marian is becoming well known. _____
2. Alyse went to Marian's concert. _____
3. Her singing brings a smile to her father's face. _____
4. The director had chosen a spiritual for the chorus. _____
5. We are taking the bus to the theater. _____
6. When Marian heard the applause, she smiled. _____
7. Rebecca often comes to the music store. _____
8. Connor leaves the opera house before the last act. _____
9. Marian has felt this excitement before. _____
10. Her mother had written to tell her about the news. _____
11. Now everybody knows about Marian. _____
12. The crowds at the Metropolitan Opera House are growing. _____
13. She gave the performance of her life. _____

Directions Complete each sentence with the principal part of the given verb as indicated in ( ).

14. She _____ every letter in a wooden box. (keep/past tense)
15. Marian _____ to her family about the concert. (speak/past participle with *has*)
16. Adam _____ *Madame Butterfly* at the Opera House. (see/present tense)
17. She _____ in Norway and Sweden. (sing/present participle with *is*)
18. Her smooth voice _____ in the night air. (ring/past tense)

Verbs, Objects, and Subject Complements

Directions Write the subject complement in each sentence.

1. The ocean water tasted salty. _____
2. The wind felt strong as we sailed away from shore. _____
3. Mary is an excellent swimmer. _____
4. The sea gulls were noisy as they circled overhead. _____
5. Jill became a coach after she won the race. _____
6. The sand was warm under my feet. _____
7. Dan is the captain of that boat. _____
8. She seemed happy when we talked. _____

Directions Circle direct objects and underline any indirect objects.

9. Mark rode his bike to the gym.
10. Mother told Max and me a funny story.
11. Paul dislikes cold water and wet towels.
12. I offered him a ride to the pool.
13. Mrs. Parkinson showed her class the new stroke.
14. Chris bought his friends a pizza.
15. Pete swam laps every day after school.
16. Take an umbrella in case it rains.
17. Pat gave Mr. Graham her report.
18. Elsa walked the dog on the beach.
19. Alexa handed me my towel.
20. The children put their goggles and flippers in the storage bin.

Adjectives and Articles

Directions Underline the adjectives in the sentences once. Underline the articles twice.

1. Quiet men often make the best leaders.
2. Enthusiastic marchers followed Chávez to an enormous rally.
3. Tired workers listened to Spanish speakers.
4. Those people wanted a better life.
5. They wanted the same rights as other American citizens.
6. Joyful crowds celebrated when an agreement was reached.
7. The black eagle on that flag represented a worthy cause.
8. Landowners resisted the efforts of a persistent Chávez.
9. The last barbecue took place on an incredibly hot day.
10. Uncle Rico told the children scary stories about ghosts.
11. An elderly woman recalled a childhood spent working in the fields.
12. She did not get a good education.
13. Now she wants these children to have the opportunities she did not.
14. A silent crowd listens as she speaks about the past.

Directions Write *a, an,* or *the* to complete each sentence.

15. Wealthy landowners hoped for _____ peaceful demonstration.
16. The family made sure everyone had _____ ear of sweet corn.
17. When _____ grapes are ripe, they must be harvested.
18. César Chávez loved living on _____ family's ranch.
19. _____ farmer might work hard and still lose his farm.
20. Chávez had _____ plan for migrant workers.
21. Men, women, and children worked long hours in _____ fields.
22. It was not _____ easy job, and it did not pay well.

Name _____

Demonstrative Adjectives

Directions Underline the word in ( ) that completes each sentence correctly.

1. Nothing grows on (that, those) high plains.
2. (These, This) animals drink from the river.
3. The giraffe is running from (that there, that) leopard.
4. Rhino wanted to migrate to (those, that) lands beyond the mountain.
5. (These, This) antelope is part of (that, those) herd.
6. I have walked through (them, these) meadows before.
7. (This, That) forest over there is dense and lush.
8. (These, Those) flowers I am holding are wild daisies.
9. (This here, This) river is swifter and deeper.
10. The hedgehog did not migrate with (this, those) animals.

Directions Write the sentences correctly.

11. This here herd is traveling over the mountains.

_____

_____

12. Them stories make me want to see Africa.

_____

_____

13. A play about the myth was performed by those there students.

_____

_____

14. That there gibbon anxiously watched the viper.

_____

15. Heavy rain fell from them clouds.

_____

Name: Sebastian Mazzini

Gold
EXTRA PRACTICE

Comparative and Superlative Adjectives

Directions Write the comparative and superlative forms of each adjective.

Adjective	Comparative	Superlative
white	1. whiter	2. whitest
busy	3. busier	4. busiest
hot	5. hotter	6. hottest
pleasant	7. more pleasant	8. most pleasant
bad	9. worse	10. worst
fascinating	11. more fascinating	12. most fascinating
colorful	13. more colorful	14. most colorful
little	15. less	16. least

Directions Circle the correct form of the adjective in each sentence.

17. This necklace is (**shinier**, more shinier) than that necklace.

18. That large ring looked (beautifuler, **more beautiful**) than the small one.

19. Of all the women, Sarah wore the (**finest**, most finer) jewelry.

20. A gold setting is (expensiver, **more expensive**) than a silver one.

21. The (**biggest**, bigger) gold mines in the world are not located in the United States.

22. California had one of the (**most famous**, famousest) gold rushes in history.

23. Gold is one of the (popularest, **most popular**) materials for jewelry making.

24. Wiping with a soft cloth is the (most good, **best**) way to clean gold jewelry.

25. Jan and I panned for gold, and I found a (largest, **larger**) nugget than she did.

26. Gold is one of the (**most valuable**, valuablest) ores in the world.

Grammar and Writing Practice Book   Unit 5 Week 4

Adverbs

Directions Underline the adverb or adverbs in each sentence.

1. He read the ancient manuscript <u>carefully</u>.
2. We will open the new library <u>tomorrow</u>.
3. On nice days the scholars sit <u>outside</u> and talk <u>too</u> <u>loudly</u>.
4. My father smiled <u>happily</u> when he saw the manuscript.
5. <u>Silently</u> the ship sailed into the port.
6. We will <u>soon</u> sail to China.
7. <u>Eventually</u>, the merchants came <u>here</u> to bargain.
8. Ishaq <u>quite</u> <u>willingly</u> visited other countries.
9. <u>Finally</u>, he finished translating the manuscript.
10. The students sat <u>very</u> <u>quietly</u> and listened to the teacher.

Directions Choose the adverb in ( ) that completes the sentence correctly. Write the sentence.

11. Of all the rooms in his palace, the Caliph loved the library (more, most).

    most (to what extent)

12. He examined that box (more closely, most closely) than the other boxes from Egypt.

    more closely (to what extent)

13. The young boy studied (harder, hardest) than his friend did.

    harder (how)

14. Of the three ships, the waves pounded (most fiercely, more fiercely) on the first ship.

    most fiercly (how)

15. She translated the poem (best, better) than her teacher did.

    better (how)

Name _____

Don Quixote

EXTRA PRACTICE

Modifiers

Directions Write *adverb*, *adjective*, or *prepositional phrase* to identify each underlined modifier. Write *adjective* or *adverb* to identify how a prepositional phrase is used.

1. The knight rode <u>slowly</u> across the plain. _____

2. Señor Quexada read books <u>about knights</u>. _____

3. Don Quixote was <u>angry</u> with his foes. _____

4. Sancho Panza rode <u>on a donkey</u>. _____

5. The <u>patient</u> squire waited for his master. _____

6. <u>Everywhere</u> he went, the knight faced challenges. _____

Directions Underline the adjectives, adverbs, and prepositional phrases in each sentence. (Do not underline the articles *a*, *an*, and *the*.)

7. The noble lord greedily collected many taxes and became rich.

8. The brave knight in armor rushed blindly toward his foe.

9. The poor farmer certainly made a faithful squire for the knight.

10. Don Quixote was a citizen of the province of La Mancha in Spain.

Directions Each sentence has a misplaced modifier. Rewrite the sentence and put the modifier where it belongs.

11. Squires only served their masters, no one else.

_____
_____

12. Rusty and dented, the knight put on his armor.

_____
_____

13. Late at night Hal read about medieval castles in bed.

_____
_____

14. Don Quixote wanted to fight only the giants; no one else did.

_____
_____

Grammar and Writing Practice Book   Unit 6 Week 1 **147**

Name _____

Conjunctions

Directions Underline the correct conjunction in ( ).

1. A trumpet sounds, (or, and) the race begins.

2. The judge placed a wreath on the winner's head (after, before) the race was over.

3. I admire Athena, (or, but) Zeus is my favorite Greek god.

4. (Although, Because) the chariot lost a wheel, the driver was unharmed.

5. We can attend the foot race (but, or) the long jump.

6. (Before, After) you leave, I want to show you my medal.

7. (Before, After) the Minoans built a palace, they covered it with paintings.

8. No enemy could enter the city (because, although) it was surrounded by a wall.

9. (When, And) the Trojans dragged the horse into Troy, Greek soldiers attacked them.

10. (So, If) you look in that direction, you will see the Parthenon.

Directions Underline the conjunction in each sentence. Write *CC* if it is a coordinating conjunction and *SC* if it is a subordinating conjunction.

11. The king of Sparta was named Menelaus, and the queen was named Helen. _____

12. Alexander became king of Macedonia when he was twenty years old. _____

13. I ran in a foot race, but I did not win. _____

14. Although the Romans defeated the Greeks, the Romans adopted many Greek ideas. _____

15. Was Pericles a general or a king? _____

16. If I had to choose my favorite Greek food, it would be dolmades. _____

17. Our founders knew a great deal about Greek politics and culture. _____

18. I'm writing about Archimedes because he was a fascinating man. _____

19. I will look on the Internet before I go to the library. _____

20. Who was a playwright, Euripides or Socrates? _____

Commas

Directions Add commas where they are needed in the parts of the following letter.

1. Wednesday January 19
2. Dear Aunt Kathy
3. When I got your letter I opened it immediately.
4. You know Aunt Kathy I love your letters.
5. Yes I am looking forward to dinner at your house.
6. Can you come to my birthday party on Sunday February 19 2007?
7. It will be as much fun I promise you as last year's party.
8. Will you spend the holidays in Dallas Texas?
9. Sincerely yours
10. P.S. Our new address is 1110 Waverly Place London England.

Directions Add commas where they are needed in the sentences.

11. Since they were in public they didn't slurp their noodles.

12. Well we celebrated Dad's promotion at his favorite restaurant Pan Asian.

13. Mrs. Gleason please let me put some dumplings rice and beef on your plate.

14. The main course a spicy chicken casserole smelled wonderful and it tasted even better.

15. Well our new house a two-story colonial is located at 175 Queen Anne Road Syracuse New York.

Name _____

Quotations and Quotation Marks

Directions Write *C* in front of the sentence in each pair that uses quotation marks correctly.

1. _____ "The warriors are fleeing!" I cried.

    _____ The warriors are fleeing" I cried!

2. _____ "Will Cortes return? asked the boy.

    _____ "Will Cortes return?" asked the boy.

3. _____ My mother said, "Come with me to fetch water"

    _____ My mother said, "Come with me to fetch water."

4. _____ "The Spaniards arrived in wooden boats," explained Ms. Rich.

    _____ "The Spaniards arrived in wooden boats." explained Ms. Rich.

5. _____ He said, "The Aztecs built bridges across the lake".

    _____ He said, "The Aztecs built bridges across the lake."

6. _____ "That nobleman is very rich!" she exclaimed.

    _____ "That nobleman is very rich! she exclaimed.

7. _____ Our teacher said to study Chapter 12 in the history book.

    _____ Our teacher said "to study Chapter 12 in the history book."

8. _____ "Maybe someday, he said, "I'll be a great judge."

    _____ "Maybe someday," he said, "I'll be a great judge."

9. _____ "Come to the festival," urged Grandma. "Bring your tortillas."

    _____ "Come to the festival," urged Grandma. "bring your tortillas."

10. _____ "Over those mountains," I pointed out. "Is the lake."

    _____ "Over those mountains," I pointed out, "is the lake."

Directions Add quotation marks and other punctuation to each sentence as needed.

11. You may go to the festival said Mother after you finish your chores.

12. Who is the leader of the Spanish I asked.

13. Montezuma is a traitor said the woman because he makes peace with the Spaniards.

14. Lake Texcoco surrounds the city explains Mr. Young The mountains surround the lake.

Punctuation

Directions Add semicolons, colons, dashes, hyphens, or parentheses where they belong.

1. Many Southerners moved to the following cities Boston, Chicago, and Detroit.

2. After church was over at 115, people went to the park for a picnic.

3. The Thomas family moved to Chicago they knew people there.

4. The family from Arkansas they used to live in Little Rock moved in with their cousins.

5. The neighbors became a close knit community.

6. Black Southerners no one knows how many moved north in search of better jobs.

7. Former farmers moved to Boston they found jobs in factories.

8. My aunt, a teacher my uncle, a conductor and my cousin, a carpenter moved from Georgia to Chicago.

9. The railroad industry grew rapidly during the Great Migration. See the graph on page 25.

10. Dear Mr. Thomas Thank you for your application for employment.

11. SARAH What time is the train to Nashville?

    ALEXANDER It leaves at 104 P.M.

12. Forty four people lived in housing that was adequate for twenty five.

13. The rules included the following 1 Work begins at 700 A.M. 2 Lunch is from 1200 to 1230.

    3 Work ends at 400 P.M.

14. The church soloists were Adam, a bass Thomas, a tenor and Chloe a soprano.

15. Eighty nine families arrived in Boston by train. For population figures, see page 236.

Standardized Test Preparation

Unit Writing Lessons

WRITING WORKSHOP — Personal Narrative

Name _____

Notes for a Personal Narrative

Directions Fill in the graphic organizer with information about the event or experience that you plan to write about.

Summary

What happened? _____

When? _____

Where? _____

Who was there? _____

Details

Beginning

Middle

End

Personal Narrative

WRITING WORKSHOP — UNIT 1

Name _____

Write a Strong Story Opener

Make the first sentence of your personal narrative an "attention-grabber." Below are ideas to help you attract your reader's attention.

Directions Write an attention-grabbing opening sentence (based on your chosen experience) using each idea. One of the sentences you write can serve as the beginning of your personal narrative.

Ask a question (Example: How could I have been so clumsy?)

_____

Use an exclamation (Example: Look out below!)

_____

Use a sound word (Example: Crack! After hearing that sound, I knew my leg was broken.)

_____

Use alliteration (Example: There I was, flying, falling, floating to the ground.)

_____

Hint at the ending (Example: I often wondered how people walked with crutches. Now I know.)

_____
_____

Make a list (Example: I felt my fingers slipping, my body falling, and my bone snapping.)

_____
_____

Set the scene (Example: My hands moved across the warm metal bars of the jungle gym on a sunny, breezy summer afternoon.)

_____
_____

Grammar and Writing Practice Book

WRITING WORKSHOP

Personal Narrative

Name _____

Elaboration
Combine Sentences

> When you write, you can elaborate by combining short, choppy simple sentences to make compound sentences. The two sentences you combine must be related in some way. You can combine the sentences using the word *and, but,* or *or*.

Directions Use *and, but,* or *or* to combine the pairs of sentences. Remember to punctuate the new compound sentence correctly.

1. I wanted to play outside. The rain clouds were gathering.

   _____

   _____

2. The jungle gym was painted bright green. The merry-go-round was blue.

   _____

   _____

3. Don't climb too high. You may fall.

   _____

   _____

4. The sun was very hot. My hands were sweating.

   _____

   _____

5. The crutches were hard to use. I figured out how to do it.

   _____

   _____

Personal Narrative   **WRITING WORKSHOP** **UNIT 1**

Name _____

Self-Evaluation Guide
Personal Narrative

Directions Think about the final draft of your personal narrative. Then rate yourself on a scale of from 4 to 1 (4 is the highest) on each writing trait. After you fill out the chart, answer the questions.

Writing Traits	4	3	2	1
Focus/Ideas				
Organization/Paragraphs				
Voice				
Word Choice				
Sentences				
Conventions				

1. What is the best part of your personal narrative?

   _____
   _____
   _____
   _____
   _____

2. Write one thing you would change about this personal narrative if you had the chance to write it again.

   _____
   _____
   _____
   _____
   _____

Grammar and Writing Practice Book

Writing Workshop — How-to Report

Name _____

How-to Chart

Directions Fill in the graphic organizer with information about your project.

Explain Task _____

_____

_____

Materials _____

_____

_____

Introduction _____

_____

_____

_____

Steps _____

_____

_____

_____

_____

_____

Conclusion _____

_____

_____

How-to Report

WRITING WORKSHOP — UNIT 2

Name _____

Time-Order Words

Directions Rewrite each sentence to make the sequence of the steps clearer. Use more than one sentence. Use time-order words such as *first, next, then, last,* and *finally*.

1. Angelina took everything off her bed, got clean sheets out of the closet, and made up the bed with pillows and a cover after she put the sheets on the bed.

   _____
   _____
   _____
   _____
   _____

2. When going down a slide you must climb the ladder, sit down at the top and slide down, making sure your feet land on the ground.

   _____
   _____
   _____
   _____
   _____

3. After Sylvia decided to make pancakes, she heated the griddle, added ingredients, mixed, poured the batter, and flipped the pancakes until they were fully cooked.

   _____
   _____
   _____
   _____
   _____

Grammar and Writing Practice Book

UNIT 2 WRITING WORKSHOP

How-to Report

Name _____

Elaboration

Use Strong Verbs

> Strong verbs can express your ideas accurately and vividly.
> **Not Vivid**   I could tell her mood by the way she walked along.
> **Vivid**   I could tell her mood by the way she trudged along.

Directions Choose the verb in ( ) that gives a more vivid picture. Write the sentence.

1. Alma (ran, sprinted) toward the finish line.

2. Fireworks (exploded, went off) in the distance.

3. Thunder (rumbled, sounded) before the rain began.

4. Did you (scrape, hurt) your knee on the sidewalk?

5. Lemonade (fell, trickled) down Sara's chin.

6. Ms. Welk has (stalked, gone) out of the meeting.

Directions Describe an animal moving or doing something. Use strong verbs such as *pounce, prowl, wiggle, scamper, lunge, gobble, yelp,* or your own strong verbs.

How-to Report

WRITING WORKSHOP

UNIT 2

Name _____

Self-Evaluation Guide

How-to Report

Directions Think about the final draft of your how-to report. Then rate yourself on a scale of from 4 to 1 (4 is the highest) on each writing trait. After you fill out the chart, answer the questions.

Writing Traits	4	3	2	1
Focus/Ideas				
Organization/Paragraphs				
Voice				
Word Choice				
Sentences				
Conventions				

1. What is the best part of your how-to report?

   _____
   _____
   _____
   _____
   _____

2. Write one thing you would change about this how-to report if you had the chance to write it again.

   _____
   _____
   _____
   _____
   _____

Grammar and Writing Practice Book   Unit 2 **167**

WRITING WORKSHOP

Compare and Contrast Essay

Name _____

Venn Diagram

Directions Fill in the Venn diagram with similarities and differences about the two people or characters you are comparing and contrasting.

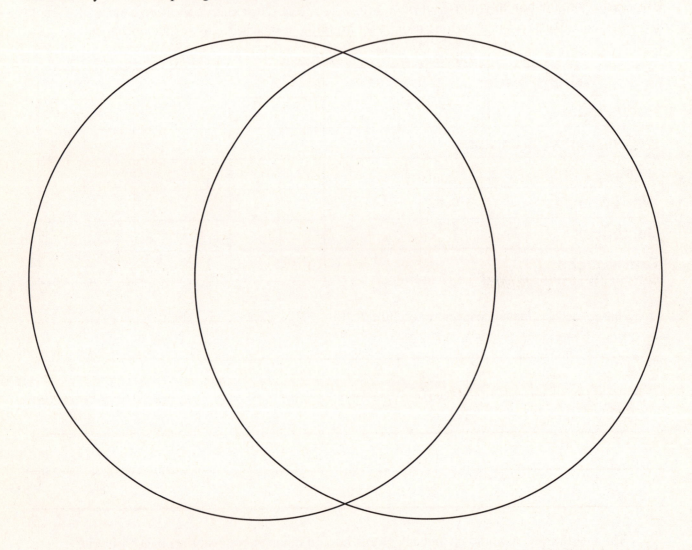

Compare and Contrast Essay

WRITING WORKSHOP

UNIT 3

Name _____

Words That Compare and Contrast

Directions The box shows words that compare and contrast. Write two sentences that tell how the two people or characters you chose are alike. Write two sentences that tell how they are different. Use words from the box in your sentences.

Likeness	Difference
and	but
also	however
too	unlike
as well	on the other hand
similarly	yet
both	
like	

How the two people or characters are alike

1. _____

_____

_____

2. _____

_____

_____

How the two people or characters are different

3. _____

_____

_____

4. _____

_____

_____

Grammar and Writing Practice Book

UNIT 3 WRITING WORKSHOP

Compare and Contrast Essay

Name _____

Elaboration

Prepositional Phrases

> You can add information to sentences by adding **prepositional phrases**.
> *Example:* The boy climbed.
> The boy <u>in the tattered shirt</u> climbed <u>on the examining table</u>.

Directions Add one or more prepositional phrases to each sentence to make it more specific. Underline each prepositional phrase.

1. The doctor gave the child a checkup.

   _____

   _____

2. The singer impressed her audience.

   _____

   _____

3. The scientist made a discovery.

   _____

   _____

4. The universities admitted women students.

   _____

   _____

5. Women achieved their goals.

   _____

   _____

6. Women have many role models.

   _____

   _____

Compare and Contrast Essay

WRITING WORKSHOP — UNIT 3

Name _____

Self-Evaluation Guide
Compare and Contrast Essay

Directions Think about the final draft of your compare and contrast essay. Then rate yourself on a scale from 4 to 1 (4 is the highest) on each writing trait. After you fill out the chart, answer the questions.

Writing Traits	4	3	2	1
Focus/Ideas				
Organization/Paragraphs				
Voice				
Word Choice				
Sentences				
Conventions				

1. What is the best part of your compare and contrast essay?

   _____
   _____
   _____
   _____
   _____

2. Write one thing you would change about this compare and contrast essay if you had the chance to write it again.

   _____
   _____
   _____
   _____
   _____

Grammar and Writing Practice Book — Unit 3 **171**

UNIT 4 WRITING WORKSHOP

Story

Name _____

Story Chart

Directions Fill in the graphic organizer with information about your story.

Title

Characters

Setting

Events

Solution

Good Beginnings

Directions Below are some different ways to begin a story. Write an opening sentence or sentences using each idea. You can use one of your beginnings in your story.

Ask a Question (*Example:* Have you ever done something that you almost instantly regretted doing? That's how I felt when I accepted this job.)

_____

_____

_____

Use a Sound Word or an Exclamation (*Example:* Watch out! The loose rocks slid out from under my feet, and I almost slipped over the edge.)

_____

_____

_____

Set the Scene (*Example:* It was a bitterly cold December day. My surroundings looked more like an Arctic wasteland than a Midwestern suburb.)

_____

_____

_____

Use Humor (*Example:* I looked ridiculous in the chicken costume. It was so big that the head covered most of my body, and I could barely walk.)

_____

_____

Use Foreshadowing (*Example:* I thought nothing would keep me from going to Antarctica. I guess I was wrong.)

_____

_____

WRITING WORKSHOP

Story

Name _____

Elaboration

Using *Who* and *Whom*

> You can use clauses beginning with *who* and *whom* to add specific details to sentences. You can also use these clauses to combine short, related sentences. Remember to use *who* as a subject in a clause and *whom* as a direct object or the object of a preposition.
>
> **General**   I talked with the man.
> **Specific**   I talked with the man who explored the South Pole.
> **Choppy**   The man has written a book. I traveled with him.
> **Smooth**   The man with whom I traveled has written a book.

Directions Combine each pair of sentences. Make the second sentence into a clause beginning with *who* or *whom* and add it to the first sentence. Write the new sentence.

1. Explorers began sailing around the world in the 1400s. They had a spirit of adventure.

   _____

   _____

2. The two women set out to explore the Grand Canyon. They were experienced hikers.

   _____

   _____

3. The man has traveled to many islands in the South Pacific. I admire him.

   _____

   _____

4. The divers have often viewed the ocean floor. We spoke with them.

   _____

   _____

5. The pilot has been around the world many times. She has been flying for 20 years.

   _____

   _____

Story — WRITING WORKSHOP — UNIT 4

Name _____

Self-Evaluation Guide

Story

Directions Think about the final draft of your story. Then rate yourself on a scale from 4 to 1 (4 is the highest) on each writing trait. After you fill out the chart, answer the questions.

Writing Traits	4	3	2	1
Focus/Ideas				
Organization/Paragraphs				
Voice				
Word Choice				
Sentences				
Conventions				

1. What is the best part of your story?

   _____
   _____
   _____
   _____

2. Write one thing you would change about this story if you had the chance to write it again.

   _____
   _____
   _____
   _____

Grammar and Writing Practice Book   Unit 4 **175**

WRITING WORKSHOP — UNIT 5

Persuasive Argument

Name _____

Persuasion Chart

Directions Fill in the graphic organizer with information about your persuasive argument.

Introduction: State your opinion or goals.

↓

First reason

↓

Second reason

↓

Third reason (most important)

↓

Conclusion

Grammar and Writing Practice Book

Persuasive Argument

WRITING WORKSHOP — UNIT 5

Name _____

Persuasive Words

Directions Write a sentence about your topic using each persuasive word below. Consider using these sentences in the draft of your persuasive argument.

1. important

   _____
   _____
   _____

2. best

   _____
   _____
   _____

3. worst

   _____
   _____
   _____

4. never

   _____
   _____
   _____

5. must

   _____
   _____
   _____

Grammar and Writing Practice Book — Unit 5 **177**

UNIT 5 WRITING WORKSHOP

Persuasive Argument

Name _____

Elaboration
Adjectives

> One way to elaborate is to use vivid adjectives. They clarify information and can often strengthen a persuasive argument.
> **General**   The state has oil in its reserves.
> **Improved**   The state has abundant oil in its reserves.

Directions Add a word from the box or your own adjective to describe the underlined word in each sentence. Write the new sentence.

| magnificent | ambitious | economical | scarce | valuable |

1. The Southwest is conserving supplies of water.

   _____
   _____

2. People went west to search for gold.

   _____
   _____

3. Even garbage is a resource.

   _____
   _____

4. Mud has been used to build structures.

   _____
   _____

5. Scientists look for ways to conserve energy.

   _____
   _____

PERSUASIVE ARGUMENT — **WRITING WORKSHOP** — **UNIT 5**

Name _____

Self-Evaluation Guide
Persuasive Argument

Directions Think about the final draft of your persuasive argument. Then rate yourself on a scale from 4 to 1 (4 is the highest) on each writing trait. After you fill out the chart, answer the questions.

Writing Traits	4	3	2	1
Focus/Ideas				
Organization/Paragraphs				
Voice				
Word Choice				
Sentences				
Conventions				

1. What is the most convincing reason in your persuasive argument? Why?

_____
_____
_____
_____

2. What part of your persuasive argument would you add more support to if you had the chance to write it again? What would you add?

_____
_____
_____
_____

Grammar and Writing Practice Book — Unit 5

WRITING WORKSHOP

Research Report

Name _____

K-W-L Chart

Fill out this K-W-L chart to help you organize your ideas.

Topic _____

What I **K**now	What I **W**ant to Know	What I **L**earned

Controlling Question _____

Grammar and Writing Practice Book

Research Report

WRITING WORKSHOP

UNIT 6

Name _____

Topic and Detail Sentences

Directions Think about the organization of your research report. Write a topic sentence and at least two detail sentences for each paragraph.

Paragraph 1
Topic Sentence _____
_____

Detail Sentences _____
_____
_____
_____

Paragraph 2
Topic Sentence _____
_____

Detail Sentences _____
_____
_____
_____

Paragraph 3
Topic Sentence _____
_____

Detail Sentences _____
_____
_____
_____

Paragraph 4
Topic Sentence _____
_____

Detail Sentences _____
_____
_____
_____

Grammar and Writing Practice Book

Elaboration
Modifiers

> One way to elaborate is to add modifiers such as adjectives, adverbs, and prepositional phrases to describe, or modify, other words in a sentence.
> **Not Elaborated**   Pharaohs built tombs.
> **Elaborated**   Pharaohs in ancient Egypt usually built costly tombs.

Directions Add a word or phrase from the box or your own adjective, adverb, or prepositional phrase to describe the underlined word in each sentence. Write the new sentence.

> year-round   fashionable   with its white marble columns
> skilled   of tropical birds

1. The Aztecs used feathers in their headdresses.

2. Ancient Egyptian men and women wore many accessories.

3. The ancient Greeks ate bread, beans, and olives.

4. Notice the design of the Parthenon.

5. The Egyptian pyramids were built by architects and engineers.

Research Report

WRITING WORKSHOP — UNIT 6

Name _____

Self-Evaluation Guide

Research Report

Directions Think about the final draft of your research report. Then rate yourself on a scale from 4 to 1 (4 is the highest) on each writing trait. After you fill out the chart, answer the questions.

Writing Traits	4	3	2	1
Focus/Ideas				
Organization/Paragraphs				
Voice				
Word Choice				
Sentences				
Conventions				

1. What is the best part of your report?

   _____
   _____
   _____
   _____
   _____

2. What part of your research report would you change if you had the chance to write it again? How would you change it?

   _____
   _____
   _____
   _____
   _____

Grammar and Writing Practice Book — Unit 6 **183**